Empowering Your Child
Who Has Special Needs

Empowering Your Child
Who Has Special Needs

Debbie Salter Goodwin

BEACON HILL PRESS
OF KANSAS CITY

Copyright 2006
by Debbie Salter Goodwin and Beacon Hill Press of Kansas City

ISBN-13: 978-0-8341-2258-1
ISBN-10: 0-8341-2258-8

Printed in the
United States of America

Cover Design: JR Caines
Interior Design: Sharon Page

Library of Congress Cataloging-in-Publication Data

Goodwin, Debbie Salter.
  Empowering your child who has special needs / Debbie Salter Goodwin.
    p. cm.
    ISBN-13: 978-0-8341-2258-1 (pbk.)
    ISBN-10: 0-8341-2258-8 (pbk.)
  1. Parents of children with disabilities—Religious life. 2. Parenting—Religious aspects—Christianity. I. Title.

  BV4596.P35G66 2006
  248.8'45—dc22

                                                              2006016949

10 9 8 7 6 5 4 3 2 1

To Lisa, our smile from God.
You continue to prove that life in Christ
is not a disabled life.

Acknowledgments

The journey to raise a special-needs child is not a solo journey. Neither is writing a book about it. I will always be grateful to Beacon Hill Press of Kansas City director Bonnie Perry, who gave me the opportunity to put words to our empowering journey. Judi Perry has once again supported me with her helpful nudges and careful editing.

I especially appreciate the parents who shared their personal insights, grief, and joys. Thanks also to the adults who shared their experiences growing up. You give us all renewed hope.

To Mark, my husband, friend, and partner in parenting, "Thank you" is a limp expression to respond to your support.

To you who read these words, share them with other parents, and make empowerment your way of life, I wish we could meet. What an invigorating circle it would be! You are my heroes.

Contents

Introduction

We're part of a circle of some of the most tenacious, courageous, optimistic, creative, persevering parents who exist. We parent special-needs children. It's not better or worse—it's just different.

One writer compares it to the experience of buying a ticket to Italy and purchasing all the travel guides to help make the most of the trip—only to end up in Holland. It's not a bad place to be. It's just not what you expected. And you need new resources to make the most of it.

That's what I hope this book is for you: a resource. It won't tell you all you need to know about raising your special-needs child. It can't cover all shapes and sizes of every special need. But it has a focus you won't find in other resources: the recognition that life empowered by God is never disabled.

I have also learned that behind every special-needs child is a parent with special needs. You have unique needs for love, understanding, support, and encouragement. Your heart has been broken more than once and will probably break again. You need to hear from other parents who alternately struggle and succeed in this convoluted journey. You need to know that you can make it. You need to know that God will help you.

Will you take an empowering journey with me? It's

a journey that seeks to discover the life God has planned for your child. It requires brutal honesty and new strategies. It also requires stepping out of the way for God to show you what He can do. Everyone wins with empowerment.

Welcome to Holland!

Something to Live With

This can't be happening to me.
What could I have done to prevent it?
—Norma, parent

The pain of one child's disability
reshapes every life in unexpected ways.
—Helen Featherstone, *A Difference in the Family*

Lisa reached for the car door handle as I released her seat belt. She made the hard scoot toward the edge of the seat and pulled on the metal handle with a few grunts. The door opened, but that was only the first step. Now she had to push it open. It took three hard pushes before the heavy door budged. Next, she worked small side steps to move her feet toward the door. A few more scoots, and one leg was out. Another hefty push, and the other foot found ground. That allowed gravity to pull the rest of her body out of the car and into a standing position.

I sat in the car, as I did every time this happened, feeling frustrated, helpless, in an internal war. Should I help or not? Sometimes I did. I would put the car in park, get out of the driver's seat, walk around to her side, open the door, release her seat belt, and let her use my hands for leverage to get her out of the car in a more timely fashion. I'm sure the long line of parents waiting to drop off their schoolchildren appreciated it. But I always wondered. Was I helping her or myself? Was making life easier her goal or mine? And what were the implications for the future? What would she do when I wasn't around?

That's when I began thinking about empowerment issues. I never used the word, but I understood the goal. Lisa needed to learn how to deal with life without my cues or all-too-quick interventions. She needed to learn what she could handle in spite of the unique set of limitations in her life.

Our story

It wasn't the way her father or I had envisioned her life. Lisa smiled her way into my heart when I accepted her father's proposal to marry "them," as Lisa always described it. Her mother, Mark's first wife, died too young, when Lisa was three and a half. From the beginning, I knew Lisa had some physical issues. She had been on medication to control a seizure problem for about a year. She moved slowly and complained of aching legs,

Something to Live With

waking up multiple times during the night. However, there was nothing that signaled the complicated, unpredictable, and confusing journey we would all take in the years to come.

Just three months into our marriage and adjustment as a family, Lisa's neurologist suggested hospitalization to find the cause for unexplained muscle weakness. We all feared a debilitating, life-threatening, degenerative disease. I'll never forget the night before we left for the hospital. I couldn't sleep. I walked to the patio window, hoping it would give me the distance I needed from the bedrooms to muffle my sobs. I was scared about everything I didn't know and might find out. I cried to God for help. I rehearsed what He already knew that I did not: what the tests would reveal, what would happen next, what our lives would be like. The more I rehearsed what He knew, the calmer I became. When I realized that God already knew what I did not and was preparing answers for all of us, I learned my most important lesson.

I don't think I realized then how critical that moment was for everything that would follow. What I understand now is that because I let God's knowledge be enough for me in that terrifying night of not knowing, it prepared me for the numberless times of uncertainty that awaited me in the future. The answer to my "What will happen?" questions is always the same: God knows, and He'll reveal the answer at the right time.

We made it through a week of difficult testing, still new at being family to each other. At the end of the week, there was a diagnosis. Besides the seizure issue, Lisa had juvenile rheumatoid arthritis. We viewed the information video that told us how we could help our child. We learned the exercises we needed to do twice daily after a warm bath. We learned about medications the doctors would prescribe. I remember the two-hour ride home from the hospital trying to process everything. At one point in our debriefing, I turned to Mark and with a great sigh of relief said, "Well, at least arthritis is something we can live with."

I didn't know how prophetic those words would become. Lisa's joint-limiting development, her daily pain, her medication and exercise regimen, her lack of endurance, her unpredictable inflammation flares, her extra doctors' appointments, and her loss of mobility were all part of the "something" to live with. Unfortunately, her challenges didn't stop with seizures and arthritis. More challenges continued to surface. There were severe learning disabilities, the depth of which was not effectively identified until late in high school. Add to that the complications that necessitated a life-threatening double heart valve replacement surgery and two hip replacements. Lisa's special needs have changed our lives *every day*. They change how we live and where we live. They change vacations. They change leisure activities. They change mealtimes. They affect *everything*.

Something to live with

That's the nature of chronic emotional, mental, and/or physical issues. They give us something to live with. Sometimes they're like shadows, dark and scary. Sometimes they offer opportunities to learn resilience and endurance we might never have learned otherwise. Sometimes they give us good reasons to celebrate small victories. But whatever they do, they don't leave us the same. In fact, they don't leave us—they're always there.

That's good news and bad news. The good news is that as parents of children dealing with a variety of chronic issues from learning disabilities to mental health issues to multiple physical challenges, we have time to learn coping, nurturing, and empowering skills. That's really very good news.

The bad news is that no matter what we do, we can't get rid of these issues. Medication and therapies may help manage them, but they don't cure them. That's why we need to learn how to live with them. One way we do that is to ask God to help us empower our children to live with their challenges. And we can't do that unless we ask God to empower us to live with the challenges as well.

To empower

- To give authority, power, or freedom to an individual

- To promote or influence self-actualization
- To give strength and inspire with confidence
- To equip or supply with an ability

From the beginning of diagnosis

From the beginning of a diagnosis, life changes. Whether or not you like it, your life has a new reality and a new set of boundaries. These boundaries affect family schedules, interactions, resources, energy, and social involvement. Learning disabilities mean tutoring and extra help with homework. A physical diagnosis means doctors' appointments, watching for symptoms, and often dealing with medication issues. A mental health issue means counseling, learning coping strategies, and balancing medication. Each changes how you expected life would be for you and your family. How do you take it all in?

> *At first we were in shock; then we faced guilt; finally our lives became all about survival.*
> —Dianne, parent

You don't. You take in only today's reality and look for ways to prepare for tomorrow. That's all you can do. There are no helpful answers for tomorrow. But God has promised enough answers for today. As the parent of a special-needs child, you have the opportunity to learn that lesson on the front line.

Something to Live With

Your heavenly Father already knows all your needs,
and he will give you all you need from day to day.
—Matt. 6:32-33, NLT

After diagnosis

Several processes are involved when beginning the journey of parenting a special-needs child. They remind us that we're part of a complicated and unfolding life. They help us realize that a myriad of responses are normal.

Discovery and confirmation. It may become apparent through recognizable symptoms, a doctor's diagnosis, or a test's confirmation. Shock often paralyzes our decision-making and processing abilities at first. Then a desire for information motivates parents to get it wherever they can: pamphlets, the library, the Internet, or others living with the same diagnosis.

A search for meaning. Questions like "What does this mean?" can easily overwhelm. Here's what I've found true. The meaning or purpose isn't in the diagnosis or disability. The meaning and purpose surface in our responses. God creates extraordinary answers in our submission. They are purposes that cannot exist without His intervention and creativity. The more confidence we have in what God wants to do in our lives *because* of our context, the more confidence we pass on to our child. Our submission to God *becomes* an empowering response.

Time to refocus. We begin to recognize that this is not just a childhood disease or crisis that will go away. We start to understand that this is long-term. It's the understanding that helps us to stop looking for some change that takes all the bad stuff away. We start asking how we need to do this. That is an empowering focus.

Assimilate and keep going. Adjustment to a chronic diagnosis is not a one-time event. Each time there is a change or new understanding, we have to find a way to accept it into our lives and keep going.

Celebrate answers and growth. Celebrate the first word, even if it comes at age 10. Celebrate the day your child puts his or her socks on without assistance, even if they're twisted. Celebrate a new attitude or trust that helps you face a new crisis without as much panic as before. A life of celebration is an empowered life.

Empowering vs. enabling

If we're going to empower our children to live life to their fullest potential, we have to begin empowering strategies early. They're not black and white. They're not one-size-fits-all. They're principles to help us consider empowering issues as we develop our parenting patterns.

This isn't just about setting goals. It may involve some goals, but empowerment is a lifestyle of various strategies. It involves how you talk about the challenges, when and why you help. It especially involves developing an affirming and secure context in which your child can

Something to Live With

learn how to deal with his or her challenges at an appropriate level of independence. It's a process of continuing education and evaluation. Empowering involves encouraging your child to act and speak for himself or herself appropriately. Empowering means preparing your child to accept the realities of his or her life.

> *Parents hold two sometimes incompatible goals: to arrange their child's world so that he feels, and is, as normal as possible, and to protect him from harm.*
>
> —Helen Featherstone,
> *A Difference in the Family*

The opposite of empowering is enabling. Enabling builds a trap for both parents and children. Enabling renders the child so self-focused that he or she has trouble fitting into a larger circle of life. It develops unnecessary patterns of dependency, which does little to prepare the child for adult life. It traps the parents into caregiving that others could and should supply.

Enabling

- Prevents or interferes with acquiring empowering skills
- Reduces a person's sense of control
- Reinforces old or nonadaptive behavior (such as procrastination or whining)

Empowering

- Promotes personal growth and increases skills
- Increases a sense of control
- Encourages new coping abilities to replace non-adaptive behavior

—Adapted from Lynchburg Area Center for
Independent Living <www.lacil.org>

I remember the pamphlet I took to heart as I began dealing with Lisa's disability. "As normal as possible," the literature kept repeating. I have come to change that phrase to "as normal as is *realistic*." It's possible to raise special-needs children with a false sense of "normal." The result does not help them adjust to a world where others have a different set of abilities. A realistic picture is absolutely necessary. That's where empowerment begins.

> *I would like people to treat me as normal as possible.* —Renea, young adult

Empowering strategies

1. Accept the realities. What you refuse to know *can* hurt you and your child more than whatever the reality is. Use any available avenue of research to identify the basic realities of your child's special needs. Don't overdose on extreme stories. Look for middle-of-the-road, basic information. If you use the Internet, use reputable

Something to Live With

sites for your primary information. Don't get basic information from someone's personal Web site. Compare
what you see and what others see in your child with the
symptom description you uncover. This helps you confront the reality picture. How is this diagnosis, these
symptoms, real for you and your family? This discovery
isn't about what you're afraid is going to happen. This is
about what's really going on. Always start there. That's
where God's help begins too.

> *It took a long time for the entire reality to set
> in and the likelihood that nothing could change
> it.*   —John, parent

2. Don't pretend. Honesty begets honesty. Be
honest with your spouse about how you're dealing with
the pressures, the fears, the unknowns, the challenges.
As it is age-appropriate, be honest with your child. God
inhabits truth, not pretense. That's why honesty about
your fears, your emotions, your endurance, your own
limitations is key. Since God already knows the whole
truth and nothing but the truth, He can help you find it
if you ask Him to.

**3. Encourage honest talk about special-needs is-
sues.** Answer any question from any family member with
the truth as you understand it. Sometimes the most
honest answer is "I don't know—we'll have to find out."
If your child believes you hide information about his or
her challenges, it increases his or her fear instead of di-

minishing it. Our kids are stronger than we give them credit for. Many times we're trying to protect ourselves when we don't encourage open and honest talk about uncomfortable challenges. Understand that I'm not suggesting that you push information on your child that he or she isn't ready for. Ask questions: *What do you understand? Do you have any questions? Did you hear anything that upsets you or makes you afraid? Could we talk about it?*

4. Adopt language that affirms, encourages, and inspires. Let me share what it doesn't mean to use language that affirms, encourages, and inspires. It doesn't mean to be positive at all costs. You and your child could face some very difficult situations. To speak positively about a negative situation won't empower anyone. To speak honestly will. To give opportunity to vent feelings so that energy can be redirected is an empowering process. To model language that helps a child express feelings is an empowering process. Use phrases like "You can," "You are," "You amaze me," "You have what it takes," "You make a difference," "I believe in you." Write them down. Slip them into daily conversation. Commit yourself to this kind of language with the same fervor you apply to medication regimens. These words empower.

Finish the following sentences for your child. Communicate at least five a day. Every week make a new list. Is it possible to run out of affirmations? Ask God for new ideas.

Something to Live With

You are _____

You will _____

You can _____

You have _____

You trust _____

You choose _____

You create _____

You enjoy _____

You know _____

5. Never do for your child what your child can do for himself or herself. Doing too much for our special-needs child is the greatest temptation most of us face. Life is harder for a child with special needs. We want to make life easier. So we overhelp. That's the opposite of empowering. We all know that sometimes we do things for our children because we're in a time crunch and it's just easier. I'm not talking about those times. I'm talking about trying to even the score by overhelping. It doesn't empower—it enables. It makes your child more dependent, not more independent. Start small, and start early. It's the story of helping the struggling chick out of the egg and rendering it helpless to survive outside its protective shell. This is not an all-or-nothing proposition. And it involves a lot of trial and error. I've done my share of overhelping. I find that it usually comes from my own guilt and discomfort concerning the challenges our Lisa faces. But overhelping enables dependence. Dependence does not help your child live life to his or her fullest potential.

> *Kids can never have any degree of independence if parents don't teach them to take care of themselves.*
> —Bruce L. Baker and Alan J. Brightman
> *Steps to Independence*

6. Be realistic about time, energy, and resources. This is just another way to look at the new realities of your life. It may take more patience, more endurance, and more physical energy to meet your child's needs on a daily basis. You're not a bad parent if you need help. Talk with your spouse or other family members who can support you. Take time away. Don't think you can meet all the needs all the time. Use whatever time management devices help you, but don't just try to get more done in a day. Sometimes you need to stop, put your feet up, and let someone else help. And sometimes you have to help your child understand that you can't meet every need, go to every meeting, and still give the support other family members need. It's another part of the reality picture. Empowerment says, *I can't do it all for you. Other people will have to learn to help, and you'll have to learn how to let them.*

7. Start somewhere. Empowering strategies evolve; they don't happen overnight. In the same way a toddler takes trial-and-error baby steps to learn to walk,

Something to Live With

you can do the same. Think about how to give your child choices. Think about how to sequence the steps for difficult skills and focus on only one of the steps. Applaud every success no matter how small. Don't wait for completed skill mastery.

Empowering questions
- How much protection does our child need?
- How much independence should we allow?
- Where should we set limits?

Learn when to give comfort, compassion, and sympathy and when to make the child quit feeling sorry for himself or herself.

—Dianne, parent

The tightrope

Empowering special-needs children is like walking a tightrope. If you protect them too much, you disable them for the future. However, if you allow too much independence too soon or without the right skills and boundaries, you set them up to fail. The good news? There's always middle ground. Find what that middle ground means for your child. It will change as age and skills change. It could change as the mental, emotional, or physical issues get better or get worse. Just commit yourself to help your child live the life God has given him or her the potential to live.

Truth brings freedom

Truth is not always the same as your opinion or perception. We can commit ourselves to a wrong perception and reject truth. Early in dealing with Lisa's learning problems and the labels I feared would isolate or restrict her, I reviewed John 8:32, which became my basic philosophy: *You will know the truth, and the truth will set you free* (John 8:32).

Using this verse, I constantly ask God to help me sift through impressions, observations, and information in order to know what's true. Sometimes God has counseled me to defer judgment about what I'm hearing or seeing until other details surface. I want to act on truth. I want to build empowering strategies based on what's true. Only God can help me do that. His truth always empowers and always frees.

Not impossible

Does it sound like an impossible journey? It's not. Empowering is an exciting, rewarding, affirming, and God-pleasing journey. It means increasing your trust in God's love for you and your child. It means the difference between struggle and freedom. It isn't a panacea that gets rid of all the difficulties and fears. However, with an empowering focus, even difficult times have new meaning.

Will you join me in this journey to learn what empowering means in your life as a parent and what it could mean in the life of your child? Remember—it's a

Something to Live With

journey toward freedom. That's God's gift for anything you must give up along the way.

Empowering questions

1. What do you do for your child to make things easier? Does this empower or enable?
2. What experience or activity have you denied your child because of your fear? Did this empower or enable?
3. What behavior do you overlook because life is harder for your child? Does this empower or enable?

Empowering strategies

- Accept the realities.
- Don't pretend.
- Encourage honest talk about special-needs issues.
- Adopt language that affirms, encourages, and inspires.
- Never do for your child what your child can do for himself or herself.
- Be realistic about time, energy, and resources.
- Start somewhere.

An empowering prayer

Dear God,

You knew the challenges my child would face from the moment of conception and before. While this reality has changed our lives in ways I don't even understand, there's nothing about it that surprises you. Thank you for your empowering words: "Do not be afraid," "I am with you always," "Nothing is impossible with me," "Do not let your heart be troubled," "I am the way," and so many more. Empower me to be your instrument of hope and stability in the life of my child.

I pray this in the power of the One who broke through life and death for me and who will do the same for my child.

Amen.

The truth will set you free.
—John 8:32

Something to
Grieve

Everything changed—the way we traveled, went places, and attended church.
—Heather, parent

While grief is fresh, every attempt to divert only irritates.
—Samuel Johnson

I always called it "the cloud." It would surface unpredictably, or so I thought. It changed my responses, my energy, my perspective, my attitude. Routine activities became major energy drains. Everything Lisa did frustrated me. I wanted to withdraw from people, from family, from life. It was a palpable shadow.

For a long time I didn't know what brought on "the cloud." I blamed it on getting too busy, missing devotions, or just having a bad day. I saw myself as incompetent, unproductive, and ineffective. Nothing I did pushed "the cloud" away. Then one day, it just seemed to be gone.

It wasn't until I attended a national conference with other families struggling with the implications of living with a special-needs child that I identified "the cloud"—it was grief. I learned that parents of children with chronic issues repeatedly find themselves somewhere in the grief cycle because they're always losing something: a dream, a piece of health, predictability, some definition of *normal,* or mobility. The list of possibilities is endless.

> *Parents of children with chronic issues repeatedly find themselves somewhere in the grief cycle, because they're always losing something.*

It's more than a response to an initial diagnosis. It surprises you in an exchange with a teacher or at a doctor's appointment or when you try to plan a vacation or a night away. You realize that life isn't what you expected it would be. Something is harder or different or complicated or missing. Something can't be fixed. The appropriate response to such change and loss is grief. It can be anything from mild sadness to boiling frustration that borders on or becomes anger to full-blown, dark-cloud depression. The healthy goal is to acknowledge it and work through it to a place of acceptance and empowerment.

The grief spiral

There are several models for tracking and describing grief. For me, the spiral image works well, because

Something to Grieve

The grief spiral

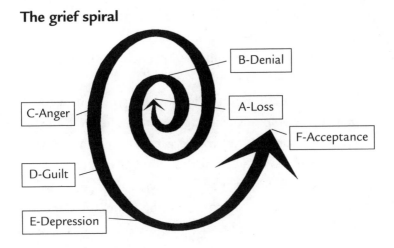

dealing with loss in the life of a chronically ill or disabled child is an ongoing process. The very definition of *chronic* means that the symptoms, the problems, the challenges don't go away. You carry them like an American Express card—never leaving home without them. The spiral communicates this static process. To identify stages and facets of this kind of grief, I use the words that best describe the experiences of parents with special-needs children: *loss, denial, anger, guilt, depression,* and *acceptance.*

Grief counselors will reiterate that responding to loss is a uniquely personal experience. While there may be a sequence that reflects an average process, there's no one-size-fits-all model for grief. You may experience one or two or all of the stages in one period of time and a different set at another time. You may experience them in this order or in another sequence. The issue is not the stages or the sequence. The issue is to deal with loss in a healthy way. The issue is to move toward acceptance, enabling you to make empowering decisions in your life and in the life of your child.

Notice that it is not a downward spiral. The arrow points up as you move into acceptance. However, the nature of a spiral is that you revisit the stages. You make the loop only to find yourself touching places you've been before. But it's not an empty visit. There are new lessons there. It's a constant learning curve, the same and different all at once.

A critical part of empowerment

Emotionally unhealthy responses to loss will not help you or your child. Getting stuck in denial or anger or guilt or depression will skew your decisions, responses, and support. To help your child respond appropriately to whatever his or her challenges are, you first have to learn emotionally and spiritually healthy responses. When you model how you're dealing with loss in realistic and healthy ways, you can help your child do the same. When your goal is to move toward acceptance, you're in a better position to make empowering decisions.

Loss

It starts with loss. It could be the loss of a dream, mobility, health, convenience, time. And it can extend more deeply. The loss can attack your security, control,

Something to Grieve

and identity. You can't parent the way you thought you
would. You have to do things in a different way. At first
it feels overwhelming and impossible. You may lose confidence and perspective.

> *I felt frustrated because I couldn't do most
> things. I couldn't drive a car.*
> —Renea, young adult

Of course it's possible to confront a loss, accept it,
and move on. It's also normal to go through different
stages as you make adjustments in your thinking, feeling,
and actions. When you recognize this ongoing vulnerability to loss, you're less likely to think of yourself as a
helpless victim and more ready to take positive, healthy
action.

Parents on Loss

> *The hardest part is their inability to have
> much of a relationship with other kids.*
> —John

> *I would say his biggest loss was an enjoyable
> elementary school experience.*   —Lynne

> *I had to give up college and a career in order
> to care for my daughter.*   —Dianne

First it was no friends at school, then no col-
lege, probably no marriage, and most certainly
no grandchildren.   —Debbie

Denial

When something happens that we aren't prepared
to process, our mind protects us by sending us into a
sort of pause mode. It's a way of coping with something
that's just too difficult to handle at the moment. We explain away what we're afraid to see. At the beginning of
dealing with a new loss, this is completely normal. If it
continues, it perpetuates an artificial perspective that
has little resemblance to reality.

This happened to me when the first signs of the
deeper nature of Lisa's physical involvement began to
surface. It came to light in the middle of our wedding.
When Lisa joined us at the altar for a family prayer of
commitment, she struggled to kneel. I remember thinking, *Why is it taking her so long?* She stretched her legs out
restlessly, trying to position them using her upper body
more than her legs. I quickly dismissed the information,
because I couldn't process the possibility that something
could be wrong. Not on my wedding day! Later, as other
symptoms surfaced, I put away denial. If I wanted to
help Lisa, I couldn't get stuck in denial.

How do you move from denial? Information helps.
Find out about symptoms and the diagnosis from reputable sources. Try on educational labels and diagnoses

Something to Grieve

to see if there's any truth in them. Look for symptoms to surface in all areas of life. See if a treatment or strategy addresses symptoms or problems. Get objective opinions. Ask questions. Don't assume anything.

Danger signs that you're stuck in denial include any of the following: You won't listen to anyone else. Every specialist is wrong. You keep searching for someone to tell you something different. You reject patterns that point out something you don't want to acknowledge.

Moving through denial
- Ask the Holy Spirit to guide you to truth.
- Be concerned if you're the *only* one right.
- Join a support group of parents dealing with similar issues.
- Get other people's input.
- Don't debate or argue.
- Ask what others see that you may not be seeing.
- Ask yourself if you're trying to deny the truth.
- Don't refuse help that could verify truth.

Perhaps you aren't caught in the trap of denying any part of the challenges you and your child are facing. There are two other responses it's possible to deny at great expense to ourselves and our families.

Anger

Anger floats into our lives as an iceberg. There's usually much more beneath the surface than ever shows.

That's what makes it easy to deny. *Anger* is such a bad word in our society that we don't want to acknowledge anything in our responses that might be close to it. In many experiences with loss, our emotions may have moved to anger, but our mind still denies it.

Anger is an emotional response to something that disturbs you, scares you, or threatens your security or control. As an emotion, it's neither good nor bad. What matters is how we release it, whether intentionally or unintentionally. Internally, a release can range from mild irritation to rage. Externally, it can involve anything from gritting your teeth to telling off the unsuspecting receptionist in the doctor's office. Unexpressed and/or unacknowledged anger turned inward because of denial plays havoc with your body and relationships. Denying it takes away your power to move through it.

So what could you be angry about? That life is unfair for your child and you? That caring for a special-needs child saps your energy, and you can't do what you want anymore? That your friends or family don't understand even though they say they do? That the medical or educational community doesn't understand your child the way you want them to? That there isn't a pill or treatment that will take this away? The list is endless.

One outgrowth of anger is blaming. Blaming seeks a target for the emotion. Anything or anyone will do. It's easier to blame your child's teacher for what your child isn't accomplishing than to accept that he or she can't do better. It's easier to blame the doctor for not prescribing the right medication than understanding what

Something to Grieve

an imperfect resource medication might be. It's easier to blame your child for not trying harder than to accept that trying harder won't take away the problem. Blaming separates people at all the wrong times.

> *Blaming separates people at all the wrong times.*

To eliminate blaming behavior, you need to honestly assess responsibility issues. Be realistic about what different support people and services can do. The school can't make up for every learning gap your child experiences. Medicine is not the perfect science we want it to be. Be careful about pushing others to accept responsibility that's too heavy for you to carry. Blaming may come from the painful realization that you can't do enough to make life better for your child. That's the loss *you* have to grieve.

Another outgrowth of anger is resentment. You resent how other family members don't understand. You resent how your children or spouse don't see obvious ways to help. You resent a complicated insurance system. You resent that activities easy for others are difficult or impossible for your family. It's critical to acknowledge anger-turned-resentment, because it saps valuable energy you need for empowering strategies.

Resentment—
comes from the French word *sentir,* which means to feel or perceive.

Re is a prefix that means again and again.

To resent is to feel the pain again and again.

Resentment is a cover-up for deeper pain. The person or issue you resent doesn't have as much responsibility for your pain as you would like to think. Resentment keeps you from going to the root of the problem. Resentment is anger misplaced.

> *Resentment is anger misplaced.*

To move through resentment requires taking off the lid and looking deeper. What am I angry and upset about? Acknowledge the hurt, the unfairness, the fear. Ask God to move into that place of hurt with His healing, compassion, understanding, and empowering resources.

Anger, with its family of multiple responses, is easy to deny. It's a master of disguise. Unmask it. Be vulnerable. God has healing for pain. He doesn't heal our cover-ups.

> *God has healing for pain. He doesn't heal our cover-ups.*

Moving through anger

- Acknowledge anger as a red-flag emotion that signals a problem.
- Give yourself permission to be angry about uncontrollable circumstances.

Something to Grieve

- Release angry feelings without hurting yourself or another person.
- Find a friend who will let you vent.
- Participate in physical activity.
- Talk to someone who has been through something similar.

Guilt

Guilt is another mask for anger. Guilt tries to make you the culprit so that you can punish yourself. If you can convince yourself that you're to blame, you can mask your real pain. It gives you sideline activity that doesn't help you see the real picture. You spend emotional energy trying to feel bad or better about something you can't control. Maybe you feel guilty because it was probably your genes, lack of resources, choosing the wrong doctor, or the medicine you took or didn't take. These are dead-end runs, because nothing in that list changes the present reality.

There's another level of guilt that sometimes affects special-needs parents. You can feel guilty because your child has more challenges than you or others his or her age do. That guilt can push you to make things easier, which seems fairer to a guilt-ridden person. However, it's a serious obstacle to empowerment. You're taking power away from your child when you act out of your own guilt. And here's why: Guilt is about you and not about your child. Guilt focuses on your pain and not your child's.

Guilt is about you and your pain and not about your child.

Guilt plays the "shoulda-oughta" game. "I should be able to do better." "I ought to organize time better." "I should be more patient." "I ought to find something that helps." Whatever you think your child needs to fill some gap in his or her life, you're not filling it—that's what makes you feel guilty. Guilt comes from setting unrealistic expectations and realizing you didn't meet them. Guilt will always hold you back from empowering steps, because it's all about *you* and *your* control and *your* help and *your* ability to make things better. Instead, you need to move through guilt so that you can support a process that makes your child stronger instead of more dependent.

Moving through guilt
- Admit feelings of guilt.
- Try to identify the source of these feelings.
- Write down your "shoulda-oughta" statements.
- Evaluate how much realistic control you have in each area.
- Ask God for wisdom about each challenge that concerns you.

Depression

Depression is that "cloud" I talked about at the beginning. You can't shake a sadness that envelops you. Ac-

Something to Grieve

tivities that usually interest you feel meaningless. You try to escape activities, whether it's shopping or eating or sports or work. An overpowering fatigue attacks your motivation. Self-blaming increases. You're on edge, and anything could knock you off balance. You feel as if someone closed the curtains on your day. You're depressed.

Most people experience periods of depression with one or more of these symptoms, especially in connection with traumatic and/or stressful changes. Parents of special-needs children are always one appointment or some new symptom away from another change or loss. The unpredictability of these changes challenges our ability to cope. Our desire for stability fights against what seems like constant change. It feels like a battle we can't win.

Depression disengages us from a perception of life that's too complicated. Depression signals *your* need for healing. Men and women may respond differently to these periods of gray days. That's important for every couple to keep in mind. Don't assume that what meets needs in one person will accomplish the same in another.

What helps?

Sometimes it helps just to acknowledge that you're in a new stage of grief that will not last. Instead of fighting against it, let routine take over. Protect yourself from major decisions or projects. Make it a priority to do one thing that stills your soul, and realigns your focus toward God instead of toward feelings. Ask God to protect you from rehearsing things that deepen sadness, especially things over which you have no control. The sadness, overwhelming feelings, dark-cloud day—whatever you want to call it—usually subsides. You know that you're going in the right direction if the sadness and lethargy are less the next day and even less the next.

Understand that you need help to deal with depression that lasts more than two weeks or if you contemplate anything that would injure yourself or anyone else. Speak with a pastor or counselor, or talk to a friend who can help you connect to some kind of professional help.

Prayer and depression

Depression isn't something you can just pray away. But you can pray about depression. Pray for God to reveal your broken perspective. Pray to connect with God's ability to see the big picture. Pray to rest your spirit with the One who invited the "weary and burdened." Pray to ask God to help you see where He *is* working. Pray for strength, patience, perseverance. Then wait for His answers to surface. They could be very different from what you think you need.

> *Depression is a cry of the soul that something is missing.*   —Anonymous

Moving through depression
- Admit your sad feelings.

Something to Grieve

- Don't use depression to excuse or rationalize in-appropriate behavior.
- Talk about your feelings with a spiritually mature person.
- Instead of rehearsing what you can't do, identify what you *can* do, and do it.
- Don't isolate yourself. Participate in activities outside your house.
- Ask for help even if you have to hire it.
- Get appropriate sleep.
- Don't neglect good nutrition at *every* meal.
- Use a journal or the computer to write out your feelings.
- Read psalms where David expresses his anguish but ends with affirmations of faith.
- Pray that God's perspective will replace yours, and be patient until it does.

Acceptance

Acceptance is the goal. This is the place where empowerment begins. You have a new reality picture. You have at least one way you're going to deal with the change or new challenge. You come to realize that nothing is "the" answer and accept each new possibility as "an" answer. You don't deny what's hard or discouraging. You know there are questions about the future that no one can answer. It's not just a positive attitude—it's deeper than that. You have allowed hope in God's picture to begin to grow in you. You're letting Him paint your picture with His ideas of beauty and balance and fulfillment. You've come to a place where you can make a difference.

> *The first thought was that something would change. It took a long time for the reality to set in—that nothing could change it.*
>
> —John, parent

Moving into acceptance

- Accept your loss without denial.
- Understand where this challenge, change, or loss fits into your life.
- Set new goals, making sure they fit reality.
- Change your questions from why to how, and receive God's answers.
- Commit yourself to "new normal," understanding that this, too, may change.

The grief spiral and children

I had already keyed into the fact that Lisa had unexpressed grief because of her mother's death. Lisa was just three and a half when her mother died. She wasn't able to work through her grief at that age. I looked for her readiness to deal with her unexpressed grief. However, I have to admit that I wasn't as vigilant in dealing with the pieces of her life she kept losing as more disability issues surfaced.

Something to Grieve

We set our patterns of how we grieve in child-hood. —Ira J. Tanner, *The Gift of Grief*

Children grieve, and not just by exploding into tears. Depending on their level of concept development and communication, they may or may not be able to identify what's going on. That's where we come in. We offer opportunities for them to explore their feelings, to name them, to express them, and to move through any part of grief and loss they experience. Sometimes in an effort to help our children see opportunities for growth, we belittle their loss without meaning to. Instead, we first need to understand the loss from their perspective.

Secure your oxygen mask first

Flight attendants always remind us that if the cabin pressure drops and supplemental oxygen is needed, we need to secure our own oxygen masks first and then help secure our children's or those of others who need help. Only a person who has a good oxygen source can help someone who doesn't. The same is true in grief work. As you process your grief and loss, you collect the tools and experience for supporting your child.

Some questions

Besides applying the possible stages of a grief spiral to children's attitudes and behavior, also use the following questions to evaluate your child's grief process:

1. Does your child demonstrate physical signs of repressed anger? Stomachaches or headaches not associated with physical causes but closely connected with a negative experience could signal your child's inability to talk about a loss. For example, if your child always complains of a stomachache on the way to a doctor's appointment, perhaps he or she struggles with what will happen there.

2. Does your child deny something you know to be true? Instead of forcing a reality check, gently search for fears or loss. Ask questions to help your child see realities. Then give your child time to process a new thought or perspective.

3. Does your child have unexplained or uncharacteristic outbursts or difficult behavior? Anger is often a cry for help. A child may not have the vocabulary or skills to voice a fear or loss. Set clear boundaries in this area. "You may say anything you feel, but you may not hurt someone else with your words or actions." We have to give our children permission to express their anger in appropriate and emotionally healthy ways. Children will not learn how to do this unless you model it first.

4. Does your child have nightmares that seem suspiciously close to a loss or fear in real life? Of course, not all bad dreams speak of loss. However, a child who experiences loss and doesn't talk about it is pushing feelings inside. They have to come out somehow and may surface in the form of dreams or nightmares.

Something to Grieve

Louann McBride is an adult who knows about childhood grief. Born without a fully developed arm, she grew up with a prosthetic "hook." Today she's a sensitive and positive presence in hospital rooms where she ministers as a hospital chaplain. She wrote of her own grief experience when she met with parents whose new baby was born with only one arm. Her words remind us that childhood grief continues to surface:

When Does the Child Grieve?
Parents weep as their healthy
Almost perfect child is born without an arm.
Long before ultrasound and without explanation:
10 toes, 2 feet, 5 fingers—one arm.
A dream shattered.
When does the child grieve?

She becomes accustomed to doing things differently
In school, at play, in sports.
Good. Good enough.
Exceptional, some would say. Perhaps extraordinary.
Certainly not ordinary. Never ordinary.
When does the child grieve?

There are the looks, the stares, the glances;
All perceived and noticed
Along with the choice to ignore and excel.
To be strong and unafraid. To push forward.
When does the child grieve?

Is it when a child first crawls across the floor
With elbows instead of dimpled hands?
Or when pattycake and hand-clapping give way
To hide-and-seek and blind man's bluff?

Is it when a young child without arms
Finds inclusion in her daycare circle
Because her storyteller teacher
Invites children to look at her hook,
Take turns touching it,
And finds confidence in similarity?
Is that when the child grieves?

I think it is when the adult
Unwraps a beautiful newborn bundle
And looks at a baby whose arms are just like hers.
Then, the child grieves.
—Louann McBride

Helping your child grieve

- Ask questions. "Did something upset you or make you afraid?"
- Give opportunities to express feelings, but don't push.
- Create an affirming family atmosphere in which a child is free to express feelings.
- Play the "I feel _____" game. Take turns at the dinner table filling in the blank. Affirm everyone who expresses feelings without making an accusation.

- Talk about feelings that aren't related to physical or learning problems.

- Regularly spend one-on-one time with your child doing a favorite activity. Use the time to freely discuss how things are going.

- Share how you deal with anger without hurting another person with words or actions.

- Use free art activities to process emotions.

- Ask your teacher or school librarian for books about children who deal with change, challenges, or loss. Read them together and talk about them.

- Read a biography about how a person transformed a difficulty into an opportunity.

- Realize that you can't grieve *for* your child but you can grieve *with* your child.

- Don't try to make the loss seem unimportant. Treat your child's perception with dignity and gentleness.

- Always answer a child's questions with age-appropriate honesty and information.

- Practice listening to your child. Don't let your words and explanations keep your child from talking.

- Make your home and your arms a safe place to land—always.

More than a picture

Once I asked Lisa to draw a picture of her arthritis.

She drew a black circle with some straight black spokes and some sprawling, tangling tentacles. It told me what she could not: that some of her challenges were predictable but many were not. I started engaging her in conversations about the things that were most unpredictable. I couldn't answer her "What will happen?" questions. However, I could give her an opportunity to express her fears and reassure her that we would be there for her no matter what. Sometimes it gave me an opportunity to put to rest an unnecessary fear. For example, since her mother died of cancer, Lisa was afraid that the arthritis was just a warning that she would die of cancer too. While I didn't know what would happen at the end of her life, I could tell her that arthritis didn't mean cancer.

Grief isn't the last word

I know it sounds as though parenting a special-needs child is all about grief. It isn't. It *could* be part of the journey. It shouldn't define it. Children are much more resilient and adaptive than we give them credit for. We're usually way behind them in processing our grief. As we understand that parenting a special-needs child makes us vulnerable to grief, we can more quickly find our place on the grief spiral, acknowledge it, and use suggested strategies to move through it. Even addressing grief in growth-producing ways is something to celebrate. And every victory counts.

Something to Grieve

Empowering questions

1. What signs of loss and grief do I see in our family responses and interactions?
2. How do I express my loss in ways different from those of my spouse?
3. How does my child grieve?
4. How can I support my child in his or her grief process?

Empowering strategies

- Don't deny grief.
- Know the stages of grief, and seek to recognize when they surface in your life.
- Support each family member's grief process.
- Model healthy ways to express grief and/or anger.
- When overwhelmed, ask for help.

An empowering prayer

Dear God,

You are all compassion, and I am all hurt and fear. You are all hope, and I have run out. How I need your help as I process information about our uncertain future! I come to you with my heavy heart and broken dreams to exchange my weakness for your strength. I will lay down my questions for today. I will not ask you for answers—just peace. Prince of Peace, take over my heart, and bring the healing I need for today. In Jesus' name I pray.

Amen.

A crown of beauty instead of ashes, the oil of gladness
instead of mourning, and a garment of praise
instead of a spirit of despair.
—Isa. 61:3

Balancing
Family Needs

The more normal our family functions, the better for the whole family unit.
—Heather, parent

To balance life, you have to know when to let go and when to pull back.
—Bell Hooks

Parenting is always a balancing act. Even in the best of situations, we don't always balance well. Add illness, a move, a job change, divorce, or a special-needs child, and everything is off-balance. That's the nature of crisis. It changes the playing field.

From the moment of birth or diagnosis, the "special" issue rearranges the family experience in some way. Whether it adds unpredictable behavior, restricted diet, adaptive equipment, medication, school challenges, or extra doctors' appointments, the family has to accommodate an increased amount of change and challenge.

The important thing is to choose the solutions that empower without adding more imbalance.

> *Balancing the demands of . . . normal life against the demands of the disability may be the hardest task of all.*
> —Helen Featherstone, *A Difference in the Family*

Unfortunately, it's very easy to make the special-needs child the center of the family's world. When you do, you tip the whole family out of balance. It also perpetuates the unreality that the whole world can revolve around one child's needs. That's not an empowering activity. Not only does it create a dependent child, but it also produces a self-centered, spoiled child.

I saw this up close in a situation that developed where our daughter, Lisa, lives. One young woman was making her solo-living debut and was completely unprepared for it. It was obvious that people in her world had tried very hard to make life easy for her—too easy. She didn't understand boundaries like closed doors and other people's food. Lisa finally had to withdraw her efforts to befriend her because of the problems she caused. It was very sad and completely unnecessary.

While it's important to accommodate special needs within the family, you have to be careful that it doesn't skew the family focus. When you focus on making life as normal as possible for a special-needs child, you can make life anything *but* normal for the rest of the family.

Balancing Family Needs

Being family isn't about meeting one set of needs. It's about becoming something together that one person can't achieve alone.

Balance is the key. Balance creates an environment for empowering. Balance protects spouses from neglecting their marriage. Balance keeps each child a priority. The problem of living off-balance is that it takes *more* energy to deal with the result of neglecting one part of family life to focus on another.

> *Conventional wisdom holds that if parents deal with a child's handicap in an open, loving, matter-of-fact manner, brothers and sisters will follow suit.*
> —Helen Featherstone, *A Difference in the Family*

God wants the family to be an affirming place to learn how to live God's way in all of life. The family with a child who has significant physical, mental, or emotional issues has an opportunity to give that child a place to learn security, confidence, and independence in safe and appropriate ways. It's a positive lesson for everyone.

Creating family balance

- Don't overindulge a special-needs child.
- Don't try to make up for what a disability takes away from a child.
- Spend one-on-one time with each child regularly.

- Explain that fair isn't equal.
- Keep family members involved in as much normal life as meets everyone's needs.
- Protect time with your spouse.
- Teach the special-needs child how to deal with second and even last place, because nobody can always be first.
- Take time for yourself. You have special needs too!
- Nurture each person's place in the family based on personhood, not needs or even helpfulness.
- Treat children as children, not as free caregivers.
- Give siblings choices as you enlist their help in caring for their brother or sister.
- Find ways to put the needs and wants of each child first at some time.

> *If parents fail to overcome some of the barriers to participation in what might be called mainstream pleasure, the resulting sense of isolation can poison their lives.*
> —Helen Featherstone, *A Difference in the Family*

The sibling effect

One of the most telling pieces of information I read when Lisa was first diagnosed was that the siblings of a special-needs child might be the more isolated members

Balancing Family Needs

of a family. Parents may overlook the needs of children who develop more normally in their parental push to meet the needs of a child with special challenges.

While no one can predict how a sibling will respond, you should be aware of some pitfalls. The most common danger in a family is that other relationships and needs become casualties in the struggle to meet the needs of one person. Other children may seek a parent's attention by taking on extra responsibilities in caring for a special-needs brother or sister.

> *Able siblings are often expected to cope and flourish with less parental attention, forcing them to manage alone with the bevy of emotions they experience growing up with a child with special needs.*
> —Wakefield Press

There are also important strengths. The most common strength is that brothers and sisters learn to be more compassionate, sensitive, and responsible in ways that help each other. They learn about teamwork and how reaching a goal together is a sweet victory.

> *Our other three children grew up more tolerant of those with special needs.*
> —Sally, parent

How do siblings respond to a brother or sister with special needs? As I have talked with parents and researched disability issues, the following are the responses that surfaced most frequently.

1. "I don't want to burden my parents." Children aren't blind. They know when things are tense for their parents. They compare their needs to the special challenges of a sibling and decide to work things out on their own. To a certain extent, this is good. However, when this happens over and over, they can grow up believing that their needs are always less important than someone else's. They become pleasers in ways that don't nurture their true selves. The biggest danger is that they become vulnerable to the first person who makes up for this attention deficit. To protect against this, find ways to tell each child that you value his or her feelings. Ask open-ended questions, and encourage honest responses. Schedule one-on-one time regularly with each child, not just for crisis intervention.

> *My biggest surprise was when I found out that you were struggling with my disability. You handled it so well that I never figured out that you were struggling like I was.*
>
> —Lisa, young adult

2. "I feel guilty being normal." It's difficult for siblings to articulate that they feel guilty being normal. They feel that something is unfair but don't know what to do about it. It's the old "Why me?" versus "Why *not*

Balancing Family Needs

me?" debate. These questions have no helpful answers in this life. The empowering truth is to build on the life you have. It's time to confront perceptions if your children try to hide or belittle their abilities, especially around a special-needs brother or sister. Talk about the definition of *normal*. Define it to mean the way God created each of us. Help your children see how the challenges one child faces gives everyone else in the family opportunities to use their strengths. Let your children hear you affirm their abilities.

3. "My brother [sister] embarrasses me." Strange outbursts. Inappropriate talk in public. Other people's stares. Each family must find ways to deal with the predictable factors of living with extra challenges. Pay attention to the responses of all of your children during these difficult times. If the siblings of a special-needs child start rejecting public outings with their brother or sister, consider it a danger sign. Acknowledge your children's feelings, and help them identify healthy ways to respond. Know when to help a child cope and when to allow absence. Develop family outings that respect each person's feelings. Make sure that you don't ignore inappropriate behavior just because you don't know what to do.

4. "It's not fair." It really *isn't* fair usually. Just make sure that no child uses this statement, "It's not fair," to excuse personal responsibility. Instead, teach the concept that fair doesn't always mean equal. Help your children ask, "What's right for this situation or this person?" "Fair" divides jobs, space, time in the right way for each person.

5. "Why don't we do things together like other families?" It doesn't happen all the time, but occasionally families withdraw from social situations because the challenges of dealing with a special-needs child are just too great. It may be the right decision for the parents, but it's usually an isolating decision for other members of the family. The goal should be to involve the whole family in as much normal life as possible. It doesn't mean that every activity is an "all play." Sometimes it means Dad supervises an outing. Sometimes Mom does. Find out what's important to your children, and creatively work to keep them involved socially with their peers and other families.

6. "Do I have to be like my brother [sister] to get your attention?" All children need attention. Some need more than others, and it may have nothing to do with a physical, mental, or emotional diagnosis. It's easy for the other children in a family to realize that the child with the greatest needs gets the most attention. It can push a child to make himself or herself more needy to get more attention. While the process is artificial, the need is real. Find ways to respond to the need for individual attention. Remember—it's all about your child's perception, not just yours. You may be able to point to ways that each child receives your attention. However, if a child perceives it differently, that's where the problem

Balancing Family Needs

is. Talk to your child, and find out what would make a difference. It could be as small as changing seating arrangements or being sure you make the next game or school event.

Thankfully, not everything is negative for the siblings of a special-needs child. There are unique positives. Growing up in a family with a special-needs child gives children an opportunity to deal with life's unpredictability in positive ways. They learn the importance of taking responsibility for helping the family run smoothly. They often have increased opportunities for independence. They learn patience. The most-often-listed strengths are increased compassion and sensitivity. The first time they protect a sibling from undeserved teasing, they become includers. As their comfort levels increase, they reach out to others who are isolated for unnecessary reasons. They come to appreciate the power of their influence on the life of another. These character-building experiences foster leadership skills, which is another benefit. As long as parents make these experiences age-appropriate, don't abuse them, and work to meet all essential needs, siblings often speak of growing up with a "special" brother or sister with more positives than negatives.

> *We've used our son's situation to teach our other children about disabilities and how God uses them in many different ways.*
> —Lynne, parent

What siblings want their parents to know

- We need you to support our right to our own lives.

- We need to talk about our feelings—the good *and* the bad ones.

- We need you to protect us from trying to compensate for our sibling's special needs.

- We need you to support normal brother-sister relationships that will probably include conflict, even with our special-needs sibling.

- We need you to expect the best from *all* of us, not just those of us who are developing typically.

- We need you to provide an emotionally and physically safe home for us.

- We may need to spend time with other siblings who live with a brother or sister with special needs.

- We need to be included in the plans you make for the future of our brother or sister.

- We need you to be *our* parents too!

- We need your presence and support at our special celebrations and achievements.

   —adapted from "The Sibling Project" <www.thearc.org>

Nurturing positive sibling relationships

- Help children see similarities, not just differences or special needs.

- Rehearse with your children how to respond to teasing or unexpected questions about their brother's or sister's special needs.

Balancing Family Needs

- Develop a family plan that protects each child's privacy and belongings.
- Give honest and age-appropriate information about their brother's or sister's special issues.
- Encourage children to express their feelings without hurting anyone.
- Ask for family input as you plan public outings.
- Reinforce that no one is to blame.

Single parents and special-needs children

What is an understandably big challenge for two parents becomes immeasurably bigger for a single parent. Cut the home support in half. Double all the nurturing, household, and financial responsibilities. The equation between needs and resources never completely resolves itself.

That doesn't mean it's hopeless—it's just different. Single parents have to find support and resources beyond themselves. At a time when you feel the most vulnerable, you have to ask for help. It feels so unfair. But remember: fair isn't equal. Make a childcare swap with another family. Investigate respite care options. Connect with another family to give your child male or female interaction. Don't suffer alone. Don't use your single parent status as an excuse for what you're not doing. Simplify your life as much as possible.

Marriage pressures

Parenting a special-needs child presents an opportunity to strengthen a marriage and also provides the context for uncovering weaknesses that already exist. Crisis always reveals what's there and what isn't. A challenge by itself doesn't have the power to make you into people you aren't. It gives you an opportunity to grow deeper, stronger, better, wiser. But it doesn't happen automatically. That's the real challenge. In the middle of a life that you didn't expect, you must protect a relationship that often falls into last place. It's easy to think that the bigger need is the family, especially the child with unique challenges. Remember—you can build a healthy family only on a strong foundation. Your marriage has to be a priority part of that foundation.

Support each other first

Do whatever it takes to make time for each other. Hire a sitter, check out respite care, use a baby monitor, or lock a door. Plan how you'll reconnect with each other at the end of busy day. Don't stop talking to each other about your dreams, your days, or your fears. Don't stop having fun with each other. Don't succumb to the lie that your marriage will make it anyway or that your child's needs are more important than your needs with each other. It's just not true. The best gift you can give your special-needs child is a strong marriage. Time invested in each other is not selfish—it's a life-saving activity for all of you.

Balancing Family Needs

An important lesson

We were at Disneyland enjoying a family vacation while in the area for a conference. Because of Lisa's endurance issues, we had to make a lot of adjustments, and her enjoyment became my priority. We rode what she wanted and ate where she wanted. During the evening fireworks, my legs went to sleep while I became her ground chair since she couldn't sit comfortably on the ground. When she went to bed, I was ready to crash. My husband, on the other hand, was ready for time with me. I raised my defenses to rationalize the off-balance approach I had adopted for this "family" vacation. But truth has a clear voice for anyone who wants to hear it. I changed my one-person priority, and we became a family on vacation again.

After that experience, I made it a priority to talk frankly about how we would reserve time for each other on vacations and at other important times. My husband has permission to tell me when I revert to unbalanced choices. It has helped me see his needs as *our* needs.

One more lesson. During the tense and time-consuming years of high school, when we all spent more time together than we wanted to, we started planning separate trips. Lisa visited a relative, and Mark and I went another direction. It was the smartest idea we ever had. Even Lisa agrees.

Protect your marriage

- Find ways to support your spouse.
- Make time for intimacy.
- Divide responsibilities to address a challenged child's daily needs.
- Always present a unified decision about discipline and activities.
- Talk about everything that troubles you.
- In the same way you schedule time for children, schedule date time with your spouse.
- Get help when you can't work through problems on your own.

Don't let discipline divide

Parents who have already decided how they will discipline, set boundaries, and protect priorities give their children a stability that's difficult to find any other way. However, finding consensus about discipline for a special-needs child is complicated. Guilt often keeps one or both parents from disciplining a "differently abled" child. It's easy to think that life is hard enough and merits ignoring tantrums. It's easy to grow accustomed to certain behaviors that are socially inappropriate. A disability does not change the principles of positive parenting and disciplining. It does, however, shape the way you use them. For example, you can't always go by the stages of normal development. Your child may develop by a different clock, sometimes very unpredictable. It

Balancing Family Needs

means that you must always match the principle to your child's ability and not just age.

> *We believe in making our child's life as normal as possible, treating him like we treat his brother with discipline, reward, and expectations.*   —Heather, parent

It took me a long time to recognize this. I would tell Lisa to straighten her room and go back to find things still on her bed and on the floor. No matter what I tried, she still would leave lots of things unattended. Unfortunately, for a long time I treated the problem as a discipline issue. Finally, I came to understand that it was part of her brain dysfunction. She couldn't process the number of instructions and the variety of actions needed to complete the task. Her brain perceived it as chaos. When I changed from discipline to skill training, it was better for both of us.

Here's the empowering truth: If your child is to live in a larger world than the confines of your home, he or she must learn to behave in socially accepted ways. Don't expect the world to accept your child's "special" behaviors the way you do. You must address appropriate behavior issues early. It's not about strictness or rules or punishment. Appropriate behavior is about taking responsibility for your actions and achieving self-discipline. It's an opportunity for children to learn consequences, cause, and effect.

Understand that many times behavior problems are symptoms of something else. Try to find out the reason for the behavior. Is it a symptom of cognitive delay? Is it a specific demonstration of the disability? Does it come from frustration or fear or being overwhelmed? Look for patterns. Research how other children with the same issues behave.

Apply the five Ws

Why does my child behave this way? *Is it part of the disability? Is it a result of ineffective parenting?*

What is my child trying to communicate with this behavior? *Could it come from fear, frustration, insecurity, anger?*

Who is responsible for making a change? *Sometimes parents need a new approach. Sometimes the child does.*

When is the negative behavior most likely to happen? *Look for patterns.*

Where does the negative behavior happen most? *Does this happen at home, away from home, or all the time?*
—adapted from Terri Mauro,
<www.specialchildren.about.com>

For a lot of our children, basic positive discipline techniques work. We just have to be consistent with them. But for other children with low cognitive development or communication problems, we have to be more

Balancing Family Needs

creative and much more persistent. This is when connecting with other parents facing similar issues can help.

More ways to address behavior issues

- Give your child a chance to communicate what he or she understands about his or her behavior.
- Identify triggers: noise, fear, insecurity, frustration, anger, changed routine.
- Teach coping skills: count to 10, close your eyes, draw a picture, listen to music, find a quiet place.
- Ask your child to finish this sentence: I feel

  _____.

- Change "Don't" statements into "You can" choices.

We all have days when there just isn't enough of us left to analyze the situation and come up with a positive strategy that meets good discipline principles. Those are our coping days. We do what we can to keep peace and make sure everyone is still alive at the end of the day. However, if every day is a coping day, there's a problem. Start somewhere. Ask another parent. Talk to a professional. Sit down with your spouse, and come up with one area where you'll begin a new strategy.

When you can't help each other

Most of the time, my down times alternate with my husband's. That's good, because one of us is usually available to support the other—but not always.

I remember one instance when I was particularly overwhelmed with the impasses at school, with medical interventions, as well as with my own sense of failure to navigate systems. I sat beside my husband heaving uncontrollable sobs. He felt completely helpless. He wanted to find solutions and make a plan. I needed someone to hear my hurt and worthless feelings. Finally, he said, "I think you need to find another woman to talk to."

At first I heard his statement as insensitive. But he was right. I needed someone to listen to my heart without feeling responsibility for my pain. Another woman *could* do it better than my husband. I came to realize that we were both reeling from different stages of grief and found ourselves at one of those precarious moments when we could not meet each other's needs because of our own gaping wounds.

Each spouse has different needs, and they don't always jigsaw together conveniently. I have found support groups helpful at times when Mark did not. On the other hand, he faithfully attended any meeting or appointment when it was important to Lisa and me. It's always give and take.

Be patient with each other when you find yourselves so preoccupied with your own stresses that you can't give what your spouse needs. Acknowledge the hurt or frustration. Build on your commitment, and move forward. Give each other space or a listening ear. Don't expect your spouse to meet all your needs unless

Balancing Family Needs

you're already meeting all your partner's needs. It works both ways.

Build a strong marriage

When spouses work together to create positive strategies, they develop a unity that is an unbeatable gift to all of their children. Just think. One other person understands what you're going through. One other person has made the same commitment to helping a challenged child reach his or her potential. One other person celebrates the small victories with you. One other person grieves each setback with you. It's the cushion that both of you need in this parenting adventure.

Have fun!

If every day is an ordeal, nobody is going to have fun at your house. Don't forget how to play. Enjoy the carefree innocence of your children, and learn from them. Plan family fun nights. Play games. Go on hikes. Have theme dinners. Have a backwards night. Light candles. Have a pajama day. Do anything that makes the day or moment special with playfulness and abandon. It will bring healing to your family. It's the medicine that doctors don't know how to prescribe even though they understand its value.

Are you having fun yet? Why not? You've heard the saying "Life is unpredictable—eat dessert first." Try it. Your children will never forget it.

Empowering questions

1. What is an example of imbalance in our family? What strategy could address it?

2. How do I purposefully make sure that no child feels neglected or taken advantage of within our family?

3. Would my spouse agree that I commit top-quality time to our marriage?

4. What positive lessons has our family learned from living with a special-needs child?

Empowering strategies

- Guard against defining your family by the needs of one child.
- Spend one-on-one time with each child.
- Promote honest communication by modeling it.
- Spend priority time with your spouse.
- Address discipline issues with positive consistency.
- Plan for fun.

An empowering prayer

Family Creator,

Our family is your idea. You have placed us together so that we can learn how to live in love. Keep us from making family about anything else. Equip us as parents to help each of our children love you, each other, and himself or herself in ways that bring about your best idea for our family.

Balancing Family Needs

*With confidence in your family design and in Jesus' name
we pray.*

Amen.

**Clothe yourselves with compassion, kindness, humility,
gentleness and patience. Bear with each other and forgive
. . . And over all these virtues put on love,
which binds them all together in perfect unity.**
—Col. 3:12-14

Surviving
School

When my son was diagnosed with learning disabilities, I felt a little shame but didn't really know why.
—Lynne, parent

Life is much less a competitive struggle for survival than a triumph of cooperation and creativity.
—Fritjof Capra

I had no idea what Lisa's kindergarten teacher was trying to tell me. She carefully measured her words as if the wrong mix could be explosive. She explained that Lisa was not showing the progress necessary for her to be successful in first grade. She suggested testing and the possibility of repeating kindergarten. I could tell she wasn't sure how I would respond. However, we had forged great trust with this experienced and compassionate teacher.

We certainly wanted the best for Lisa, and if repeating kindergarten would give her a better foundation for future success, we had no problem with it.

Then the tests came back. They confirmed that Lisa was functioning below expected standards with significant gaps. I blamed it on the emotional upheaval in her life. I blamed it on the focus-robbing arthritis pain. I blamed it on her seizure medication that could slow mental processes. I convinced myself that we could catch up next year.

But we couldn't. More tests identified severe learning problems that only complicated her physical issues from arthritis. I got the same crash course in navigating the special education system that all parents get: a pamphlet and everything the teacher could tell me before her next parent appointment.

Thus began the most arduous navigation challenge I have ever faced. During Lisa's schooling, we tried a little of everything: public school with resource room, special education self-contained classroom with appropriate mainstreaming, private school, and homeschool. Every option offered some answers as well as more problems. Nothing fit perfectly. However, as I look back, I'm able to be more objective. I can see what made a difference and what didn't matter. I can see where I tried too hard, where my perceptions were wrong, or how my own needs got in the way.

Surviving School

A proving ground

In many ways, school is a laboratory for life, but not in the way you might think. It's the first place outside home where parents have to confront differences and gaps and decide how they'll respond to them. School connects you to one of your first sets of professionals and helps you learn the communication and teamwork skills that have empowering implications. School may become the first place your child functions without you. It's where he or she learns how to ask for help and begins to solve some problems on his or her own. It gives your child a place to interact with others and learn how to deal with the negative encounters that are sure to occur.

It will always be a mixed bag, sometimes sharing strategies and tools that make a big difference, sometimes not. No matter what kind of experience it becomes, school is a learning laboratory for more than just academic skills. When you treat it that way, not every decision has to work in order to give you important information. Learning what doesn't work may be just as crucial as learning what does.

The following are five foundational understandings that should shape your involvement and influence at school in order to make empowering choices.

1. Make life, not just school, your priority. Early on I had to adjust my thinking to the big-picture focus. I had to address the fact that this could not be about Lisa's success in a set of state-mandated standards. Nor could it be about my success to fill all the gaps to make her successful. It had to be about meeting Lisa's needs for life. That meant more than just meeting her learning needs. It involved meeting social needs and self-concept needs. It involved keeping her childhood as carefree as possible.

This was why I consistently turned down Lisa's opportunity to attend extended learning opportunities through the summer. She had worked hard enough all year, and she desperately needed the break. On the other hand, another parent has told me how important a special outside-of-school tutoring program was for her son. Always evaluate opportunities based on what will make a difference in your child's *whole* life, not just school performance. Life is more than school.

2. Answers come from people, not institutions. It is easy to blame problems on the school or some other institution that can't supply answers. Institutions often don't have enough money or people or equipment to make all the difference they would like to make. There will always be shortfalls. However, the long-term answers we need for our children don't lie in an institution or program or school. The answers come from people who connect with our children, understand their needs, and creatively brainstorm concerning how to meet learning needs. When you understand this principle, you stop complaining about institutions and start learning how to work with people.

Surviving School

Of course, there will be some teachers who connect better than others. The truth is that there is a place for every person and every lesson as you confront school issues. Learning how to learn from every teacher is one of a parent's most important jobs. There's *always* something to learn.

3. The more you learn, the more you *can* learn. It took several years before I understood the importance of the principle that "The more you learn, the more you *can* learn." In fact, this truth still guides Lisa's learning today, because learning is a lifelong goal. School is only one way to achieve it. All learning counts, not just mastering math and reading comprehension. While the three R's create a strong foundation for learning, other learning is also important. Learning phone numbers, making instant pudding, problem-solving about what to do if the bus lets you off at the wrong place—mastery in these areas may never show up on any report card, but they make empowering differences in life.

The empowering lesson here is to help our children believe that the more they learn, they more they *can* learn. This isn't about accumulating facts and information. This is about embracing learning as a goal and life mission. It's about learning *how* to learn, *when* to learn, and sometimes *why*. Our job as parents is to find ways to encourage our children to help them embrace the adventure of finding out what *else* they can learn.

4. Try differently, don't just try harder. Lisa is a try-harder-to-please person. When homework was difficult or a paper came back with more X's than checks, Lisa would try harder. Quickly we learned that trying the same strategy harder wasn't going to get new results. We had to find a different strategy. For example, it took a long time for us to learn that Lisa's reading comprehension went up when someone read aloud. While we couldn't read *everything* aloud, we did a lot of reading assignments together, especially in high school.

The only time trying harder solves a learning problem is when lack of motivation is the key issue. Even then, a new strategy, a new tool, or a new person to help explain can often solve a motivation problem.

5. Always ask God for direction. God created your child. He understands every short circuit or cell malfunction. He also knows what your child needs to master for the future. And He understands your time and energy boundaries. Listen when God nudges you to stop pushing. Listen when He suggests a different priority or strategy. He's your most knowledgeable learning specialist. Let Him "direct your paths."

No matter what your child's functioning ability is, it's important for everyone to learn what makes the difference between a positive learning experience and a negative one. It's not just the teacher or the placement. Actually, you as parent have a lot more influence in the outcome than you might realize. Learning where your influence is and how to use it positively is a basic empowering strategy.

As you explore the following principles and suggestions, keep in mind the big picture. You're looking for

Surviving School

ways to empower your child to live the independent life
he or she has the potential to live. With that focus, you
can always find answers.

A parent of a special-needs child has to be a

- **Detective**—looking for clues that will unlock mysteries.
- **Coordinator**—transferring information from one professional to another.
- **Librarian**—keeping appropriate records.
- **Communicator**—helping articulate the child's needs.
- **Monitor**—evaluating progress and identifying problems.
- **Cheerleader**—encouraging every success.
- **Implementer**—helping apply new strategies at home.
- **Nurturer**—helping the child's spirit grow strong.

> —adapted from Allison Martin and Rick Martin
> <www.prematurity.org>

1. Listen first; speak last. Listening to a teacher
first gives you a better opportunity to share your perspective. Listen to what the teacher says works at school.
Let the teacher hear from you as to what works at home.
Both of you can borrow from each other's experience.
Neither of you holds the whole truth. The school offers a
specific environment for your child's learning. That
alone can account for differences between a home and
school experience. Listen to help yourself identify the
factors responsible for a change in behavior, motivation,
or performance.

Use this listening strategy with your child as well.
Nearly every time I spoke before I listened to Lisa, I made
assumptions and even jumped into wrong actions that I
regretted later. If you listen first, you can find out if your
child is frustrated, embarrassed, misunderstood, or has
a wrong or mixed-up understanding. Ask specific questions like "What did you say?" "How did that make you
feel?" or "What do you think would make it better?"

2. Help your child write a letter to the teacher.
Helping your child write a letter to his or her teacher is an
idea I picked up from the Arthritis Foundation as we en-
deavored to educate teachers about Lisa's physical need
for moving painful joints every 20 to 30 minutes. At first I
used their model. Later, Lisa and I created our own. Each
year, I asked Lisa to articulate her fears and concerns. We
brought it to the annual meeting for creating her individual educational plan. Even the process of composing the
letter was helpful. Sometimes I learned things about
Lisa's fears that I didn't know. Make sure that the letter
sounds more like your child than you. This isn't a way to
get your ideas across. Rather, it's a chance to teach your
child an appropriate way to voice feelings and frustrations. It's a good learning experience for both of you.

3. Organize for success. Most special-needs children profit from routine organization in all areas of their
lives. When I realized that Lisa couldn't problem-solve
time changes in a routine, we wrote down a time schedule—one for school days and one for the weekend. She

Surviving School

gratefully used it as a guide to help her hurry when she got behind. It took a lot of panic out of our school mornings. Learn the level of organization your child can handle independently, and supply the help he or she needs for other areas. Remember that empowering means that you don't do for your child what he or she can do for himself or herself. However, it doesn't mean to expect instant results either. Nor does it mean to frustrate your child in the process. Take it one small step at a time, and reward big.

One observation. Over and over I had to admit that these organizational processes started with me, not Lisa. Without becoming an organizational maniac, the more organized and committed to a healthy routine I was, the better we all were. It meant that I got up first, early enough to be awake and smiling by the time Lisa was up. At least that was the goal. Getting up first was easier to master than the smiling. Also, if I was organized about breakfast, lunch, or anything else that was part of my morning responsibilities, it was easier for everyone when something didn't go as planned.

4. Give your child a chance to solve problems before you step in. When there's a problem—and there *will* be problems—step back before you make a call or take action. Help your child identify and articulate whatever is at the root of the problem. Protect everybody from letting surface issues hide deeper issues. Then encourage your child to initiate communication with a teacher, by either conversation or a written note. Practice with your child how to phrase appropriate questions. Understand that your child often mirrors your own responses, so give yourself a time-out if you feel your emotional blood pressure rising.

Help your child know how to ask for help in appropriate ways. As parents, we learn the nonverbal cues our children give us. We also put up with some of their interruptions. Teachers and other specialists can't do that, because they're responsible for more children than we are. That's why we have to teach our children how to ask for help. Teach simple words that signal a problem: "I'm confused" (or scared, hurt, sick, or sad). Graduate to explanations. Even nonverbal children can use codes or signals. Helping your child communicate for himself or herself in appropriate ways is a crucial life skill, and school is a good place to learn it.

5. Look for ways to support the teacher. Volunteer in the classroom. I've offered to grade papers, spend an hour helping other children, go on a field trip, whatever I could to express my thanks for any extra time my child took. This goes past spending time in the classroom just to check up on your child, even though that's important. I've even offered a fast-food lunch when the only time a teacher could meet with me was over lunch. We both benefited.

6. Let homework show where your child struggles. Homework is not about the grade. It's about practicing new skills. It is about evaluating progress. If homework doesn't show where your child struggles, be assured that

Surviving School

the test will. The best time to address what a student doesn't understand is with homework.

I took education classes in college, and one particular lesson has been critically important as I have worked with Lisa. It had to do with a French psychologist and teacher, Jean Piaget, who spent his life listening to how children think. He listened more carefully to wrong answers than right answers. Wrong answers shared clues as to the misunderstanding or false information that produced the answer. He helped me see that wrong answers come from some kind of order in a child's mind. If I could figure out where they came from, I might be able to find a solution.

This was especially critical as I worked with Lisa in math. We tried everything to teach her the arithmetic tables. Nothing worked. Finally, I asked her to explain how she came up with the answers to addition and subtraction. I found out that she just said the first number that came into her head, because that's what she thought the other kids did. When I realized that she didn't have a number concept, I started working with ideas that focused on this missing foundation. That's when we all came to recognize that her brain dysfunction was the culprit, not her memory or her motivation or even the teaching strategy. Lisa couldn't learn arithmetic tables because it was beyond her ability. "Wrong" answers could be your most valuable clue to real problems. They uncover our assumptions about what a child understands.

When to talk to a teacher about your child's homework

- When homework takes double the expected time because of disabilities
- When your child shows signs of giving up because of frustration
- When you don't know how to help
- When your family's schedule prevents completing the assignment

Do what you can to make homework time as pleasant as possible. Find out what kind of environment helps your child focus best. Does he or she like to be where the rest of the family is? Does he or she like it quiet and free of distractions? Make an agreement with your child about homework time. Keep a time and achievement chart if you want to document a problem. Remember—homework also teaches time organization, which is an important life skill. No matter how "hard" homework might be, there are long-term life lessons your child can learn. There's always something to learn.

How to help your child with homework

- Set goals *with* your child, not *for* your child.
- Help your child recognize progress.
- Encourage with specific praise about what he or she is doing right.
- Don't show disappointment if your child doesn't achieve what you hoped.

Surviving School

- Be prepared to reteach a concept or skill.
- Connect new skills and information to daily life.
- Refer to recommended homework help Web sites.
- Help your child organize a regular homework area.
- Use a timer to schedule breaks.
- Practice retaining skills and information with games.

7. Start with established processes before asking for exceptions. It may be one of the most frustrating things you have to learn, but usually the best way to accomplish change is to start with established processes before asking for exceptions. Even when we knew that something wasn't going to work for Lisa, we still tried to "go along with the program" so that we could document it as something that needed to change. I found that it made for better teamwork and less adversarial responses. Obviously, that doesn't work where physical and/or emotional safety is at risk.

> *We found that schools were more than willing to meet us halfway when they realized that we were willing to work with them and not demand things.* —Dianne, parent

When someone suggested a new idea or placement or diagnosis, we "tried it on" to see if the remedial strategies addressed the problem. When you're trying to find out what works best, anybody could have a part of the truth you haven't discovered yet. I tried to help Lisa develop an open mind to new ideas even when it pushed her out of her comfort zone. After all, there could be some important life lessons that have nothing to do with learning style or skill mastery. It's not just about school success. It's always about life.

Understand—
- the difference between standing up for rights and being a difficult parent.
- how and when your emotions get in the way.
- the need to get the full story.
- that there could be a difference between the child at home and the child at school.

Build a positive teacher-parent partnership
- Communicate successes as well as concerns with a teacher.
- Compliment a teacher when an idea works.
- Set up an appointment if you have a concern. Don't corner a teacher.
- Let your child's homework show where your child struggles.
- Don't be a "helicopter parent," always hovering but never helping.

8. **Use school to help identify your child's character strengths as well as learning abilities.** It will be the

Surviving School

strengths of your child that will empower him or her in the future. Unfortunately, school time will probably focus on weaknesses. That's why you have to balance this with pointing out other strengths. Affirm relational strengths of sensitivity or helpfulness. Affirm enthusiasm and endurance. Affirm humor strengths when used appropriately. All of these are attitudes that will help your child through a multitude of difficult times.

> *My heart is not disabled.*
>
> —Lisa, young adult

9. Pray for your child's learning specialists. Pray for their families. Pray for their health. Don't be one-sided in your prayers. Pray for these support people in ways that don't have anything to do with you and your child. Answers to prayer have a ripple effect.

Teacher meetings

Meeting face-to-face with your child's teacher and learning specialists is essential for team-building. The appropriated time slot isn't enough to share your child's life story or yours. Nor is it a place to tell teachers how difficult life is for you or your child. The time is set aside specifically to report on your child's progress and make sure you know where the weaknesses and challenges are. Make it your priority to hear what the teacher has prepared to tell you. If you have ideas, try asking them as questions instead of making demands. Teamwork will always help you more than an adversarial relationship. An adversarial relationship quickly degenerates into a tug-of-war that's no longer about your child's best interest but is about who's winning the tug.

> *There was the uncomfortable feeling of sitting around a table with five to seven school specialists and feeling like I was in trouble. I felt like I was the only person in the school who had a child that required this much assistance!*
> —Lynne, parent

If you become known as a difficult or demanding parent, it has the potential to interfere with how much the teachers want to work with you. Even when the stakes are high enough to warrant extreme measures, look for ways to build bridges.

When you meet with a learning specialist—
- Prepare for the meeting.
- Be on time.
- Review notes from the last meeting or report.
- Think before speaking.
- Be specific about concerns without making accusations.

    Accusation: "You embarrass my child when you call on him [her]."
    Concern: "My child feels embarrassed when he [she] has to speak in front of the class."

Surviving School

- Stay focused on one issue at a time.
- Express gratitude for time, effort, or any other positive contribution.
- Share what your child likes about school.
- Don't die for the little things.
- Understand the educational process and lines of authority.
- Apologize when you're wrong or when you overreact.
- Keep an open mind.

The following ideas will help you be the kind of parent every teacher wants to work with.

1. Organize important information in a notebook or file. The paperwork it takes to maneuver your child through the educational system is mind-boggling, especially if your child receives help through an individual educational plan. Create a notebook, or buy a small file box to keep up with all the paperwork. Put a quick-see date on the first page of any group of papers you file, and *always* highlight dates. When forms look alike, it's difficult to identify which year or semester or review it is. Use a special color to mark anything you want to review before the next meeting. Use another color to mark ideas or strategies you want to use at home.

2. Review the last test or teacher's meeting or IEP before a new meeting. Make notes about what worked and what didn't work at home. No one can dispute your home observation. That's where you're the expert eyewitness. Make a short list of questions, and be prepared to ask them if the teacher doesn't cover them. If you're preparing for an individual education plan meeting, make sure you understand the order the team will follow as identified from last year's review, and organize your information and questions accordingly.

3. Be open to the teacher/team's assessment and school observations. At school the teachers and other specialists are the eyewitnesses. While their observations can be as subjective as yours, they tell you how other people perceive your child. That's crucial life information, even when you don't believe it accurately describes your child. Teamwork happens when *all* of you look for reasons for discrepancies.

> *Seek agreement with the primary people—teachers.*   —Theresa, learning specialist

4. Recruit a listener/advocate to accompany you to meetings. It's difficult and sometimes impossible to hear everything you need to hear, especially if you're already overwhelmed with meeting your child's special needs at home. Find another parent who has had experience in the educational system to accompany you as a listener and note taker. It takes a lot of pressure off you. Give this person permission to ask questions to help get helpful information. You can also pay for the professional services of an educational psychologist or independent counselor. Ask about parent advocate programs in your area. These people understand how to negotiate professionally. Their objective input can be invaluable.

Surviving School

5. When possible, both parents should attend key meetings. When I knew the decisions were especially critical, I often made sure that both my husband and I attended the meeting. Occasionally, Lisa requested her father's presence. Often he was the better listener and could ask better questions. Sometimes it was only his presence that spoke the loudest. Choose the time when it makes the most positive and helpful sense. Single parents shouldn't consider their single status as a weakness in the meeting. Teachers work with realities. So should you. The issue is to bring together all possible resources.

> *I encourage parents to quit speaking for their children. Often at meetings, parents will do all of the talking and not allow their child to be a part of the decision-making. I encourage parents and students to trust that the student has valuable insights and important opinions. The goal is to empower the student to speak for himself or herself and to empower the parents to trust the thoughts and desires of their child.* —Theresa, learning specialist

More ideas for successful teacher-parent relationships

- Think about your questions and write them down.
- Be prepared to take notes.

- Ask for examples of behavior or learning problems when you don't agree.
- Learn how to advocate for your child's realistic abilities instead of your dreams.
- Tell professionals what others have tried—what worked and what didn't.
- Keep track of who you talk to and when.
- Keep a notebook of past reviews, work samples, and resources.
- Dress to make a positive impression.
- Ask to schedule another meeting if unresolved issues remain at the end of allotted time.
- Be willing to try a new idea or strategy for an agreed-upon time.
- Leave other children at home or with a sitter.

Learning beyond school

Remember—this is about life and not just school. That means you want to make as many connections between life and school as possible.

Field trips. A field trip isn't just a school activity. Take family field trips. Check local and community newspapers as well as your city's Web site for informative, hands-on discovery museums, festivals, or other experiences. Research vacation sites, and include one or two of these kinds of learning activities in your trip. Since the best learning begins with curiosity, not grades, find

Surviving School

out what your child is interested in and capitalize on it, especially in the summer.

Play games. A number of learning and social skills are involved in playing games. Children learn how to make choices, see the big picture, follow rules, practice appropriate behavior, and problem-solve. Make games a key part of the way the whole family interacts. Stop it at the point of competition with a statement like "If we're not going to have fun, we can't play."

Read! Reading continues to be the most significant aid to learning. I always read aloud to Lisa, even in high school and beyond. I chose books that were within her interest but outside of her reading ability. We read through the whole *Chronicles of Narnia* and made it most of the way through *Les Miserables*. I always wanted her to know about the adventures waiting for her in books. Besides, she could learn how to find out things on her own if she could read. I knew I had turned a corner when Lisa brought me a book to read after she had finished it. All those trips to the library had finally paid off! Today reading is one of her favorite leisure activities, even though she still could not pass a comprehension test on the material. She reads for story and insights, and that's enough for her.

Also use audio books as another way to access literature. Check out a classic from the library for a family car trip. Allow stories to play aloud during rest times.

Connect school learning to life skills. Keep up with what

your child is learning so you can demonstrate its use in daily life. Connect current events to history. Connect fractions to cooking. Ask your child to tell you the time, count the change, make a purchase, write an item on your grocery list, answer the phone, write down information, or write to grandparents. The list is endless. Most elementary teachers provide extended learning ideas for home. Web sites are full of them. Make learning meaningful, and your child will learn what he or she can.

When you disagree with a learning specialist—

- State your disagreement without making an accusation.
- Reaffirm your belief in the teacher's desire to meet your child's learning needs.
- Support your observation with verifiable facts.
- Suggest a trial period for a new strategy or placement.
- When all else fails, get information about your right to appeal.
- Follow the designated steps without trying to manipulate or short-circuit the system.
- Pray for the right attitude, the right timing, the right people, and patience during processes that take time.

Every individual education plan paper will remind you how to make an appeal. It's a part of the system of checks and balances that's critical to our democracy. It's another way to advocate for your child's needs. Be sure that what you want to address is worth the fight. When appropriate, make sure your child agrees to the appeal. Support the teacher and your child's context during the appeal. Bad feelings won't help your child develop positive relationships with authority figures later in life. And remember—there's something wrong if it's always you and your child against the world.

School is a window for life. While home tries to adapt to the child, school helps your child adapt to others. Both are important. Understand that your child's teacher doesn't have all the answers. Neither do you. Combine your experiences, your information, and your commitment to make a difference so that you can make wonderful answers together. Then school becomes a vital part of the life lessons that will make empowering differences in the years to come.

Empowering questions

- What is your child learning about himself or herself as a lifelong learner? How can you encourage positive discoveries?
- What is school teaching you about your child's behavior and adaptive skills outside home? How can you use this information at home?
- What are you learning about yourself and your own needs as you participate in teacher conferences?
- If life is more than school, what skills do you see your child developing that will be crucial for life?

Empowering strategies

- Make life your priority.
- Look for answers from people, not institutions.
- Adopt a lifelong commitment to learning.
- Help your child to try differently, not harder.
- Listen first; speak last.
- Organize for success.
- Give your child a chance to solve a problem before you step in.
- Let your child speak for himself or herself in meetings.

An empowering prayer

Supreme Teacher,

Help me take my cues from you. You don't overwhelm me with too much information, push to be right, lecture, or need my success to make you effective. Teach me to do the same for my child. Remind me often that the mark of your life is abundance and freedom—even at school.

In the name of the Master Teacher.

Amen.

Wisdom is supreme; therefore get wisdom.
Though it cost all you have, get understanding.
—Prov. 4:7

Negotiating the Medical Maze

Our daughter has had more experiences in a doctor's office than at birthday parties and overnights.
—Debbie, parent

Tell us the truth, and if you don't know what it is, tell us that, too.
—Terri Mauro, "About Parenting Special Needs"

We were connecting to yet another pediatrician, hoping to find someone who was interested in coordinating the many aspects of Lisa's health issues. He looked at Lisa's history with a challenged interest. *This is good,* I thought. He recommended some specialists and tests that no one else had suggested. His line of reasoning seemed logical, even hopeful. I didn't even mind the complicated city drive that took us home. Finally, maybe there was someone in the medical field who could help

us through the multitude of medical issues that constantly overwhelmed us.

That's the cry of every special-needs parent. Give
me a doctor who wants to go the second mile, who
knows what to do with the health issues that complicate
our lives, someone who really listens. Today, in a medical system controlled too often by insurance plans,
finding the best doctor is not always within your control.
That makes your position as advocate very important.

> *We have been to many specialists and received
> very few answers. We have spent a lot of time
> and money and have little to show for it. All
> we know is what the boys don't have.*
>
> —John, parent

In the beginning, with birth or early diagnoses, you
are your child's voice. *You* watch for symptoms. *You* exe-
cute a medication regimen. *You* inform the church nurs-
ery or preschool about your child's needs. But when
does that change? When does your child take over
charting seizures or filling medication containers or talking to the doctor about symptoms? As early as is age-appropriate and with as many baby steps as possible.

I remember one mother who would not accept the
fact that her late adolescent had to become totally responsible for the diet and medication implications of
her diagnosis. "But she could die if I don't make sure she
does everything right," she countered. Without insensi-

Negotiating the Medical Maze

tivity to that real and imminent possibility, I tried to help her understand that unless she was going to shadow her daughter into high school and college, she had to take the beginning steps that would turn the responsibility of her daughter's health over to her daughter. She didn't, and she still endured life-threatening emergency room trips.

On one hand, every parent understands the enormous responsibility for making medical decisions that have lifelong effects. They are decisions about surgery or no surgery. They are decisions about medications and their side effects. They are decisions about tests and how far to go. They are decisions about treatments—so many decisions. Knowing when and how to bring your children into these decisions is not based solely on age. Emotional readiness is an issue. Mental abilities factor in. Always start simple, and evaluate the results. It's a critical process of training your child on how to make a health-related decision.

Part of the difficulty of dealing with medical issues has to do with the fact that we deal with chronic issues most of the time. Chronic issues never go away. Symptoms may simmer only to raise their ugly heads to bring about some new crisis. Chronic issues frustrate many doctors. They can't make our children well. They can only manage symptoms. And sometimes they can't even do that. Behind the professional and sometimes overly sterile ways often lies a gnawing frustration that nothing they've learned is good enough to help. And when it's children, it's even more frustrating.

> *An irreversible disability poses serious diffi-culties for doctors as well as parents. Physi-cians are trained to be problem-solvers.*
> —Helen Featherstone, *A Difference in the Family*

How do we raise our children to take responsibility for their health needs? It starts in very simple ways. It grows with a child's ability and desire. The following are some ways to get the process started.

1. Model responsibility in your own health choic-es. Don't expect your children to make better choices than you in areas of exercising, eating healthy, getting appropriate sleep, or following a doctor's instructions. The first place we empower our children is with our own models. Children imitate the models they see. They also grab for the snacks that are most convenient. Make sure that healthful choices are the most convenient. Find ways to put exercise into family fun. Take walks together. Play tag in the backyard. Rake leaves together. Make *to-gether* the word that has all the fun in it.

This wasn't easy for us. Lisa had limited likes and multiple dislikes on a healthful food list. I worked hard to introduce more and more healthful choices to her school lunches. However, just like everyone else, there were days that I sent what I knew she would eat. As for exercise, it became a bad word to Lisa. She had exercises

Negotiating the Medical Maze

to do three times a day. I tried to plan fun activities and not call them exercise. I bought children's exercise music and made a fool of myself trying to do it with her. When we worked in the yard, we tried to include her. Not every idea worked, and sometimes it was more time efficient to simply *do* the exercises. However, we kept trying.

2. **Teach age-appropriate understandings about limitations and treatment.** Knowledge is a part of empowerment. I used a coloring book from the Arthritis Foundation to teach Lisa why her legs hurt so much. Keep the first information very simple. Always be willing to answer any questions. Place questions to which you don't know the answers on a list for the doctor next time. Don't be surprised if children have a nonchalant attitude toward a diagnosis. Unless a diagnosis comes with specific changes, many children simply take the news in stride.

> *They have to understand themselves better than anyone else.*   —Lynne, parent

3. **Involve your child in discussions with the doctor.** Again, use age-appropriate ways to involve your child in dialogue with the doctor. It could be as simple as "Show the doctor what you learned to do this week" to "Ask the question we talked about in the car." Let your child describe symptoms to the doctor. Practice ahead of time if you need to. Or bring the list and report them the way your child communicated them to you.

Keep asking if your child understands words or processes, especially in front of the doctor. Ask your child to explain what he or she understands when you get back to the car.

Empowering your child on a doctor's visit

- Let your child describe symptoms to the doctor.
- Give your child an opportunity to answer the doctor's questions first.
- Talk with your child about an upcoming appointment. Find out what questions he or she has.
- Encourage your child to ask questions for himself or herself.
- Keep asking your child in front of medical personnel, "Do you understand?"
- Bring your child into the discussion with medical personnel.

Sometimes I would start by saying, "Lisa asked me to bring these issues up." And then when I finished, I would ask Lisa if I represented her thoughts and feelings. Most specialists go out of their way to make your child comfortable and feel included. However, I find it easy to monopolize the conversation. Empowering my child in the doctor's office is a choice, and I have to choose it over and over.

> *Include a social worker, chaplain, care coordinator, or someone else who will advocate for you and your child's needs.*
> —Louann, hospital chaplain

Negotiating the Medical Maze

The ABCD bag of tricks

Terri Mauro shares her "ABCD bag of tricks" in her e-zine for special-needs parents. She suggests that parents fill a bag with something to **A**muse, **B**ribe, **C**omfort, and **D**istract. Here are some examples of items to include: small toys, card games, flash cards, a small notepad and pen, dice, finger puppets, keys, coins, photos, hard candy, pretzels, books, puzzle books, raisins, animal crackers, a doll, a magnetic travel game, crayons, and stickers. Sometimes children are best engaged in one-on-one activities. These include simple games like 20 Questions, I Spy, Rock-Paper-Scissors, or Which Hand Is It In? You could also take a walk, get a drink from the water fountain, look out a window, whisper secrets, or take turns asking questions. You can play word games like Hangman or Boggle. Play the Three Things game by asking for three things you did yesterday, want to do today, ice cream flavors, and so on. Or play the alphabet game, finding a word for each letter. Make up several versions to keep the game new. Use the alphabet game for objects in the waiting room, names of animals, your child's toys and activities, and so on.

Keep this bag of tricks for waiting room experiences only. Update it frequently for age and interest changes. Retire some ideas to bring them back later. Make it a bottomless bag so that the child always feels there's something else to do. Make waiting room experiences bonding times instead of a test of your patience. Understand that the *normal* attention span for a child is one minute per year of age. Special-needs children may function below that norm. That means that if you're going to occupy a four-year-old for up to a 30-minute wait, you'll need at least 8 to 10 different activities. And don't forget the wait in the exam room. Your goal is not to use everything in the bag but to have what your child needs to make the doctor visit as pleasant as possible for everyone.

4. Help your child take appropriate responsibility for taking medicine. For some of our children, medication is critical to their ongoing health and relief from debilitating or uncomfortable symptoms. Most parents become very diligent in monitoring medications. What we aren't as diligent about is helping our children assume responsibility in this area. Here are some ways to train your child to take responsibility for medication.

For young children
- Use a chart and stickers.
- Connect medication to regular meals or times.
- Ask your child to remind you.

For older children
- Involve your child in filling a medication container.
- Ask your child to make a reminder chart or sign.
- Ask your child to explain each medication and when to take it.

The first empowering goal with medication is positive compliance. The next is for your child to remember

Negotiating the Medical Maze

to take medication without your cueing. Always help your child see the positive value of medication.

When medication becomes a way of life, it's easy to forget safety precautions. Keep medications out of reach of children. That may mean your child must ask you to get his or her medicine from the "safe place" where you keep it. Use safety locks, and keep them tightly in place. Keep prescription medicines in their original containers. Keep a current file of the information sheet for each medication. Make sure a responsible adult oversees taking medication.

Schools communicate their policy for administering medication. It often involves a doctor's prescription, original medication containers, and a Ziploc bag to keep it in. It's usually a good idea to duplicate this policy anytime your child must take medication away from home. When you prepare the information for school, duplicate the process, and you'll be ready for a babysitter, church outing, or evening at a friend's house.

Consider the possibility that if a child rejects responsibility for medication, it *could* be a symptom of denial. Telling him what he or she *should* do, nagging, or lecturing about what will happen without the medication won't address denial. It addresses compliance. Go back to chapter 2 and review ideas for helping your child through this step in a grief process.

5. Understand that children need extra help when a daily routine or context changes. I learned in a dramatic way that children need extra help when a daily routine or context changes. Lisa was doing well remembering to take her medication for seizure control and arthritis relief. We were using a medication container and linking her medicine schedule to meals and bedtime. However, when she stayed at a friend's house while my husband and I attended a conference, the change of place and routine threw everything off, and she "forgot" to take her bedtime medicine, which contained one of her critical doses for seizure control. Thankfully, it didn't result in seizures, but she did experience some very uncomfortable side effects for 24 hours, which knocked her out of an activity that she had looked forward to. After that, Lisa asked someone to remind her to take her medicine when she changed her context or routine. It's an empowering strategy she continues to use.

Empowering our children involves helping them take appropriate responsibility for their medication, their physical limitations, their diet, or anything else that keeps them as safe and healthy as possible. Parents who take the police-all philosophy and try to monitor everything *for* their children render them helpless. Overprotection doesn't protect. It renders our children very vulnerable.

> *It's so important for a special-needs child to advocate for himself or herself. We can advocate for only so long.*   —Lynne, **parent**

Negotiating the Medical Maze

Keeping records

How do you remember who prescribed what medications when and for what? How do you remember what medication worked and what didn't? How do you remember what test occurred when and with what results? While I have a detailed memory about the key issues of Lisa's physical issues, it's never enough to fill out the new patient information when we see a new doctor. There are several ways to keep on top of record-keeping. Choose the ones that work for you.

1. **Keep a medical notebook.** It can be as simple or complicated as you want to make it. I have one that's 8½ by 11 in which I hole-punch reports and prescription information. I quickly found that the big notebook was too bulky to carry to most appointments. I now use a pocket-sized notebook that fits in my purse or pocket. I date the doctor's visit, identify the reason for the visit, list my questions, and summarize answers, treatments, medications, or tests. That's where I summarize my personal action plan: pick up prescription, call new doctor, order suggested equipment, put reminder on my calendar about calling for next appointment. The notebook is for reports and information.

2. **Keep organized files in one place.** You can use an expanding file, a portable file box, or a section in a family file cabinet. Start with the simple divisions between school and medical. Divide each by year or other

category. A file is only as good as what you put in it. Be sure you commit yourself to the process of *filing* if you're going to keep a file. Stacked papers waiting to be filed are no help.

3. Keep the pharmacy printout or prescription insert to document medication history. The easiest way I found to track Lisa's medication history was to retain the pharmacy printout or prescription insert. I simply highlighted the name of the prescription, date, and reason it was prescribed. I would go back and highlight any side effect that she experienced, if necessary. As I prepared for a new doctor, I could review this list. Eventually, I made a computer list and updated it from time to time.

4. Request copies of reports and hospitalizations. Copies of reports and hospitalizations become invaluable. A new doctor who can peruse medical history on the first visit can address treatment issues more quickly. Occasionally, I have been asked to hand-carry reports to another doctor. I always made a copy of the reports before passing them on to the doctor. Ask your child's doctor if you can have a copy of test results. With today's requirements concerning privacy, you may have to put your request in writing. Hospitals usually charge for a copy of the hospital record.

5. Keep a one-page summary of pertinent information. When Lisa visited a relative or had a sitter, I made available a one-page summary of important information. It identified the date of each of her diagnoses

Negotiating the Medical Maze

and a current list of medications with the amount and how frequently taken. You also should include medication and food allergies. List all the names and phone numbers of doctors your child regularly sees. Date your updates. I also made a reduced copy to fit in my billfold so that I have this key information with me at all times. File the old summary to provide another way to track your child's history, doctors, and medications.

6. Keep a chronological medical history. When we moved, it was very important to have a chronological medical history. While the new doctor's office will write for medical records, it's very helpful to have something in writing for a new doctor to see. I've tried to keep a one- to two-page chronology that I can hand to a new doctor. I try to use the *Dragnet* style of reporting: "Just the facts." This isn't a time to interject your questions or concerns about another doctor's findings.

7. Ask for a copy of a new-patient information sheet. A new-patient information sheet reminds you of the information you need to take with you to a new doctor's appointment. If a medication, diagnosis, or surgery list is complicated, consider making a separate summary page to be attached. It saves a lot of time in the office.

8. Check out record-keeping software or Internet services. Some software programs and Web sites allow you to track medical information. Some provide ways for doctors and emergency rooms to access the information with your permission. The downside is that you have to enter all the information. The upside is that they offer a way to make great reports on the spot. You'll have to decide their cost-effectiveness. There are a number of technological advances in this area. Just keep searching for anything that makes tracking easier for you.

Keeping medical information

- Keep a summary chart in the front of the file to document additions.
- Keep informational files for specific diagnoses separate from medical history.
- Keep a summary sheet for hospitalizations, tests, and so on.
- Keep a summary sheet for injuries that required treatment.
- Include immunization record.
- Identify names of all doctors and health care professionals by year.
- Make a copy of the birth certificate.
- Keep test reports.
- List surgeries.
- Keep an updated list of current medications.
- Keep a list of past medications and why they were terminated.

Always take the following to each doctor's appointment:

- A printed list of current medications, specific doses, and frequency

Negotiating the Medical Maze

- A list of symptoms, changes, and/or questions
- The time of the last medication dose (in case of blood work or other tests)
- List of allergies

Add to a new doctor's appointment:
- A copy of most recent test results or X-ray
- The place and date of these tests
- All current doctors' addresses and phone numbers
- A one-page chronology of your child's medical history
- A printed list of all surgeries, along with hospital, surgeon's name, and address

Safety issues and special-needs children

Whatever strategies you learn from your community, school, and pediatrician's office, start there. However, the basics are generally not enough to keep our kids safe in a world that doesn't always understand them.
- Put ICE (**I**n **C**ase of an **E**mergency) on your cell phone. This is an emergency contact number in case you're unable to communicate for yourself.
- Find a way to attach ID to your child. There are bracelets, necklaces, and Velcro shoe tags. Make sure your child always uses it. If it's a routine part of dressing, your child will be wearing it in an emergency.

- Place emergency contact information on the back of a car seat or backpack.

I ended up in lots of pain. I went to see doctors a lot. It was hard for both my parents to see me in pain so much.   —Lisa, young adult

Empowered hope

There's a sense in which we must always live in the moment *and* in the future. We must identify the strategies and routines that keep our children healthy and safe for now. However, we must do it in a way that turns as much responsibility over to them as possible. We must bathe all of it in prayer, submitting to and trusting in our Great Physician. Then, when we've done our best and prayed our prayers, we must let God answer in His way and his time. We're powerless to make a difference without God's empowerment. He empowers us to empower our children. No doctor or test has the last word. God does. That's our lasting hope.

Empowering questions

1. How do I model healthful choices? Where do I need to start?

2. Do I have adequate medical information organized in a helpful way?

3. How can my child be more involved in doctor's visits or medication regimens?

Negotiating the Medical Maze

Empowering strategies

- Practice ideas that make your child increasingly responsible for health issues.
- Be honest about limitations or differences.
- Help your child talk to a doctor about symptoms or questions.
- Make an "ABCD bag of tricks" for doctors' visits.
- Help your child preplan medication regimens and other issues in new situations.
- Keep good records.

An empowering prayer

Lord,

Sometimes I wish someone would rescue us from the impersonal medical system that we depend on to protect our child's life. What's routine for the medical community is often crisis for us. Remind me often that I don't have to check with any insurance company to ask you to treat my child. You're our Primary Care Physician. We're in good hands.

Learning to keep appointments with you first, I pray in your name.

Amen.

I pray that all may go well with you and that you may be in good health, just as it is well with your soul.
—3 John 2, NRSV

Finding Help

I'm stubborn, and I want to do everything by myself. I don't like to ask for help. But sometimes I need help.
—Renea, young adult

Nothing makes one feel so strong as a call for help.
—George Macdonald

Help! That was my silent cry as I began the journey parenting a child with challenges outside my experience. Not only was I in charge of regular family and home matters, but now I also was Lisa's daily physical therapist, pharmacist, energy monitor, medical appointment chauffeur, and historian, as well as the one who ran back and forth from bathroom or bedroom because Lisa couldn't turn on a faucet, put on her socks, or reach her clothes. Help—that's what I wanted. But I didn't know where to get it. None of her teachers at school had ever dealt with childhood arthritis. Adaptations at church were more difficult because volunteer help could do only so much. At home I pushed through my day, always three projects behind and more than a few hours of sleep short. Where could I get help?

Early on, I had to face the fact that I could not take this journey by myself. While my husband was always supersupportive and shared the responsibility for exercises, medication, and doctors' appointments, I was the stay-at-home mom. There was never time away for me.

> *We asked ourselves, "How did this happen?"*
> *Then, I pulled up my warrior boots and got*
> *busy finding help.*   —Heather, parent

Empowering help

Why is it that we are more eager to give help than receive it? Help empowers us to give our best. Helplessness distracts and renders us ineffective. Throw away any idea that you can make it without help. You can't. You need emotional support to ward off irrational perceptions. You need the support of extra hands when yours are not enough. You always need prayer support. And sometimes you have to realize that other people may be able to help your child better than you. Accepting that truth makes you a stronger, not weaker, parent.

Finding Help

It's a vulnerable feeling to admit you need help. The tendency is to protect our places of vulnerability. We don't want to expose our need. We think that neediness is weakness. May I offer another way to look at it? If your goal is to be the parent who meets all of your child's special needs from nurturing to safety to skill development and beyond, you'll enable dependency. If your goal is to find the best help, resource, or person to meet a specific need, and you understand that it won't always be you or your idea or even your hands, then you begin to empower.

> *Do I have any power to help myself?*
> —Job 6:13

On the other hand, you can't present yourself as needy as you always feel. If you define your family by your child's special needs, answer other people's "How are you?" with the latest problem, and have difficulty with conversation that isn't about your unique circumstances, you push people away. You can overwhelm them with information they can't do anything about. Their attempts to understand do exactly the opposite for you. You end up without the help and support you desperately need.

Of course there's a balance. Finding help empowers it.

An example

I began teaching Lisa independence skills early. When we tackled purchasing items in a store, I made a difficult discovery. Lisa's painstaking struggle at the cash register to process the math as well as the physical struggle it took to produce the appropriate cash became an emotional issue for me. It forced me to confront what I didn't want to see: that life was going to be very difficult for Lisa. I found myself trying to make the process easier (for her or me?) by helping her get her money out or putting it back. I would make some supportive comment to Lisa loud enough so that it served as an unnecessary explanation to the checkout person or shopper next in line. I came to realize that until I could work through my emotional struggle, I couldn't empower Lisa in this area. When I found out that what bothered me didn't affect my husband, I asked him to take Lisa on these practice shopping trips. Later, when she started grocery shopping, we paid someone to take her once every two weeks. It was an empowering choice that helped all of us.

When it doesn't feel like help

Occasionally it seemed as though the more honest I was about our family's situation, the more I attracted the wrong kind of help. Many well-meaning people gave suggestions that didn't fit for one reason or another. It always left me feeling empty, not supported. I complicated the problem because I didn't know how to express my need in ways that gave people legitimate ways to help. They just wanted to make something better for me or Lisa or both of us. I just wanted someone to understand.

Learn how to articulate your need for help. Start with family and graduate to friends and professionals. There's help available, often just one question away.

1. Talk to a friend. Hearing the way I express how I feel helps me begin to understand where I need help. While it might seem that your spouse should be able to fill that role, usually someone else can do it better. Each parent bears his and her own silent pain. It's the unexpressed pain that prevents the help you want. Someone who doesn't deal with your issues every day can listen better. An objective observation from someone who wants the best for you could help redirect your focus, help you understand how emotions cloud a perspective, or give you an idea that might make a difference.

2. Don't hide your feelings behind your child's challenges. It's so much easier to rehearse our child's issues than to talk about our own. Why should it surprise us when people want to solve something that we talk about the most? Are you frustrated, overwhelmed, afraid, or hopeful? Say so. It opens the door to support that helps.

3. When someone asks about your child, return the favor. Full of my own challenges, I too easily became insensitive to someone else's. It takes a predetermined goal and a lot of practice to answer a friend's question about your difficulties and then ask an equally sensitive question of your friend. It's the kind of volley that protects the relationship from becoming one-sided.

4. Be specific. Our friends and family aren't mind-readers. If I'm looking for a way to solve a problem, I need to ask people for ideas. If I want someone to tell me I'm doing the right thing, I have to be willing to hear the truth.

5. Communicate needs in ways that protect your child's privacy. Some people questioned why we weren't more public about some of Lisa's issues. The answer was simple. Lisa didn't want everyone to know every detail. As a family, we talked about how to express the changes and challenges and always honored Lisa's wishes.

6. Stay grounded in the facts. Every situation has an unending list of what-ifs. Practice repeating the facts first. Those are the realities. Nobody can help you deal with what-ifs. Even God reserves His help for reality. Say, "The test results are not in," and ask for support during the waiting period. Say, "The first day of school didn't go well," and ask for a new strategy for the next day. Asking for specific help empowers us, because it forces us to deal with realities. Besides, it's the empowering skill we want to pass on to our children. If we struggle here, our children will struggle more.

7. Accept the desire to help even when the help

isn't what you wanted. People who don't live with our unpredictabilities and limitations don't fully understand. But they want to. Sometimes out of awkwardness they say things that don't feel like support. Accept their heart without evaluating their words.

Family and friends

Extended families and close friends share your joy when you bring a new child into the world. They also share your pain when you find out about a difficult diagnosis or challenge. Often they're your best support group. Other times you find that their way of helping feels more like interference. Have you asked any of the following questions?

Why don't they understand better? Maybe it's because you tell them only what you want them to know. Maybe because you hoped they would know without saying it. Maybe because they understand only what they're emotionally prepared to assimilate. Rather than expecting them to understand so they can better help, look at what motivates any attempt to help. Most of the time even awkward words come from love and concern.

I learned this as I shared Lisa's struggles with her maternal grandmother. I thought for sure she would understand automatically. She had already endured the pain of losing her only daughter, Lisa's mother. She had accepted me like a daughter-in-law. But her only answer to my search for support was simply "You'll figure out something." It left me empty. In time I came to understand that Lisa's challenges involved too much pain added to the loss of her daughter. She meant her statement to affirm her confidence in me as Lisa's new mother. When I stopped expecting her to give me what she could not, I was ready to receive what only she could give.

Why does everybody tell me how do something differently? It frustrated me more than once. Wasn't I doing my best? Did someone think I should be doing better? I shared Lisa's struggles to help them understand better. What I didn't realize is that their own helpless feelings motivated the suggestions. Again I had to be willing to accept the person's desire to help, instead of receiving their suggestions as an evaluation of my competency.

Why won't my family or friends help more? Many actually believe it when you say that you're fine. Have you asked for help? If you're unwilling to expose your need, how do you expect someone to know that it exists? Another reason family or friends are slow to offer help is because you don't set clear boundaries. They're afraid that you expect too much for too long. Ask a family member to watch your child for one hour for a quick errand. Then come back early.

About family gatherings

While family may be your best source of emotional support, family gatherings can be your worst nightmare. Many of our children don't handle changed routines,

Finding Help

multiple food choices, and the chaos. It calls for a survival plan. Adapt these ideas to fit your situation.

Surviving family gatherings

- Communicate a time limit before you go.
- Establish a signal between you and your child and/or your spouse so that you can change your plans as necessary.
- Take a change of clothes for unpredictable accidents of any kind.
- Bring one survival food item, just in case the menu doesn't work.
- Don't delegate the full responsibility of watching your child to someone else. Stay near enough to know what's happening.
- Bring a backpack with toys, pillow, utensils, medication, comfort foods, or anything else you know works.
- Bring out one item at a time.
- Watch for overstimulation, and be ready to find a quiet corner.
- Use the gathering to evaluate your child's socially appropriate behavior. Make a note of what you need to work on.

People generally want to help. But they don't want to be taken advantage of. Sometimes in our overwhelmed situations, we're so desperate for help that we fail to think of other important issues. Make the following directives part of your survival plan.

1. Always give people permission to say no.
When anyone responds out of fear, guilt, or duty, the help they give doesn't support in positive ways. Clear the air of guilt or duty. Lead with statements like "I can't ask you if you think you can't say no." That usually opens the door for honest communication. But you have to back it up. No fair reneging.

2. Don't barter emotionally. "I know you want to spend time with your grandchild, so I thought . . ." Don't play the emotional card. It will come back to bite you. Simply request the help. As much as possible, make it a win-win proposition.

3. Set boundaries. When you give time limits for childcare, keep them. Don't be late without calling. Instead of hoping that a transportation arrangement works for the whole school year, try one week or one month at a time. People are more likely to agree to help when there are clear time and responsibility boundaries.

4. Set up a co-op or trade system. It can be as simple as asking to trade out childcare for a shopping trip. It can be as organized as a plan with points. The advantage of this kind of help is that you become a helper as well as a person who is helped.

Where to find help

Can you find support that will make a difference? Can you make positive connections? Does anybody really want to help?

The answer is yes. Friends and family want to help. Support groups and agencies organize themselves to help. The Church and Christian community have a mission to help. Sometimes you have to pay for the help you need. Other times you find volunteers. No one group can fill all your gaps. Neither do you need each group all the time. The key is to know where help exists, and connect with it early enough so that it's available when you need it. The worst-case scenario is to be overwhelmed in crisis and have nowhere to go for help.

Since there's no one-size-fits-all support, families must find what meets their needs. If you're willing to admit that you need help and are willing to experiment with possible resources to find it, help is on the way. Hiding or taking the try-harder route just hurts, and overwhelmed feelings will only rob you of the energy you need.

Friends

Friends are valued traveling companions. They make long journeys more enjoyable. They make hard journeys possible. They offer objective views. They wait with us for the hard-to-hear news. They don't have to understand everything because we trust their love.

Find a friend to ask the hard questions, and listen to his or her response: *Am I too hard on myself? Do I expect too much from my child, the doctor, or the school?* Find a friend who will be a prayer partner with a quick call or e-mail and without having to know all the details. If you can unload any unnecessary fears or find help carrying the real ones, your load *is* lighter. Always be careful not to take advantage of a friend's time. Also, make sure the relationship does not become one-sided. Find ways to give back support.

I'll never forget how friends came to our support when I hit a wall of hopelessness. Someone asked me point-blank what kind of help I needed the most. Our biggest need was for transportation to and from Lisa's two-hour job. Single-handedly this friend organized a volunteer transportation schedule. Lisa enjoyed one-on-one time with a variety of people, some of whom are still involved in her life. I enjoyed waving her off and welcoming her back in a way that I had not been able to experience. As long as you remember that volunteer help is a short-term answer, you won't panic when it begins to fall apart.

Try a support group

It was at least three years after receiving Lisa's diagnosis before we ever met another family dealing with childhood arthritis. Even when we went to doctors' appointments, the clinic was for families waiting to see a variety of doctors. It left me feeling very alone. Even worse, it left Lisa feeling like an alien.

Then I read in our newspaper that the National Juvenile Arthritis Association would be conducting its annual family conference in St. Louis, where we were living at the

Finding Help

time. Immediately I registered our family. We attended workshops, heard family-friendly medical presentations, and talked with other families. Finally, Lisa saw other children with arthritis, some much worse than she, others carrying the invisible marks of the disease just as she did.

> *Parents of children with special needs are each other's greatest resource. They can provide information, inspiration, support, and understanding like no one else can.*
> —Terri Mauro, *About Parenting Special-Needs Kids*

At that conference I met another St. Louis mother who asked the same question I did: "Why don't we have a childhood arthritis support group?" We decided to organize one and began meeting once a month. That support group connected me to families in similar situations who asked the same questions, felt the same guilt, struggled with similar challenges. Even more important, Lisa played with children who had juvenile arthritis just as she did. They couldn't sit on the floor. They didn't like to do their exercises. She wasn't an alien after all.

Support groups can be a critical empowering gathering. They offer a place to talk about the daily challenges related to your child's special needs. Somebody might even have an answer to a problem that stumps you. Even if it's a gathering of parents whose children face a variety of disabilities, it still offers a level of understanding, compassion, and encouragement that no one else can give.

We have a fabulous support system in our home group. They have walked through some very deep waters with us. —Heather, parent

Support groups are especially important in the beginning of a diagnosis and during a crisis. It's normal for people to weave in and out of support groups, depending on perceived needs. The key is to know where to connect and how. Often it serves a family well to make a visit so that the connection is there, just in case they need it.

Don't be surprised if the first time you go you don't receive the help or support you expected. Support occurs as you tell your story and connect with someone else's. That takes time. It may feel that it takes more time than you have to give. It's another question of balance.

How to find a support group

- Ask for suggestions from a health care professional or school counselor.
- Make an appointment with a hospital chaplain.
- Look in the community section of your local newspaper and/or phone book.
- Research the Web.
- Ask those who supply support services to your child.
- When you identify a phone number or e-mail, ask the important questions: Who attends? How many? Where does it meet? How long does it last? When does it meet? What's the best thing you've witnessed?

Finding Help

- Visit with an open mind. Consider attending at least twice.
- Stay on the mailing list.

Consider starting a faith-based support group for parents of special-needs children. When Christian parents come together to support each other in this journey, it's an exciting, empowering circle. See the Appendix for more information.

Explore organizations and agencies

National organizations exist for many diseases, syndromes, or other life challenges. Most send informational e-mails and/or newsletters. Find out how to get on a mailing list. Their resources provide a good way to stay informed about the normal progression of a disease or challenge, to review symptoms, to read family success stories, to identify research, and to receive other practical help. Some organizations offer support groups and conferences. Know where the information is so you can access it when you need it.

Most communities offer some kind of respite care for severely challenged families. This is a way to help families who can't leave their special-needs child with anyone but a medical or experienced person. Schedule a visit. If you like what you see, take your child for a visit. Try it out for a short time before using it for several hours or an overnight visit.

Talk with a social worker through your child's

school or hospital. Social workers are unbelievable networkers. They keep up on what's available in your community to help with a variety of special needs. They're often willing to research answers to your questions. However, they can tell you only what's available. They can't tell you what will work or guarantee that what's available will solve your problem.

Over and over, special-needs families bump up against what a community isn't equipped to do. What makes sense to us doesn't make sense to an agency. Or it simply costs too much money to provide it. Every time I access help for our daughter from an agency or community resource, I have to rehearse the reality that they aren't required to solve my daughter's problem. While they can become a part of the answer, rarely do they supply everything we need or want. Keeping a reality picture here is an empowering lesson.

Teaching your child to ask for help

If you think it's hard for you to ask for help, remember that it's even harder for your child. The push for independence often makes our children believe that asking for help perpetuates dependence. It took a long time for Lisa to understand that she had adopted a limiting definition that would not empower her toward independence. She believed that independence is doing something for yourself, by yourself, and without any help. It was a definition that spelled failure. Over and over we reinforced the idea that asking for help was the most independent thing you could do. We tried to use our family life to model a definition of interdependence. Slowly, very slowly, Lisa initiated her own search for help.

> *I was afraid God would leave me like everyone else. Then I read this verse: "The Helper, the Holy Spirit, whom the Father will send in My name, He will teach you all things, and bring to your remembrance all things that I said to you" (John 14:26, NKJV). He will give me a helper! He will teach me when to do what at the right time, because He makes sure I remember all I need to.* —Lisa, young adult

In order to ask for help, a child needs to be able to identify a problem. When families adapt to behavior problems instead of using family life to practice strategies to ask for help, they send confusing messages. What will it take to help your child ask for help? Nonverbal signals, pictures, making it a family life expectation? There's a lot of security in knowing that your child will ask for help. The more comfortable your child becomes asking for help at home, the more comfortable he or she becomes asking for help away from home.

Looking to your church

Christian families look to their church for support. Sometimes they want more help than the church is equipped to give. Always start with the support your church gives to everyone. For example, they help you to understand and apply biblical lessons to any struggle. They pray for you and with you. They offer a place for fellowship with other Christians. They offer a variety of family resources and activities.

Some churches have organized very specific ways to support special-needs families. They may offer a Christian support group. They may have a special-needs Sunday School class for children who function better in a context structured to meet their needs. Some offer various kinds of respite care. Others have camps, latchkey programs, or other special activities for children or their parents. While there's a push to address this overlooked area in many churches, it may be slow to come to where you live.

Unlike the school, churches depend mostly on volunteer help and only a few paid staff members if any. If your church does not have a special-needs ministry, it's not because they don't care. Every pastor and staff juggle needs against available resources and come up short. Find out where your church can help, wants to help, has the ability to help, and let the help start there.

> *With only a few exceptions, most people at church have been supportive and tried to include [our sons] in as many activities as possible.*
> —John, parent

Finding Help

Maybe it's because I'm a pastor's wife *and* a special-needs parent, but I've never expected the church to do what it didn't have resources or personnel to do. This was never clearer than when our daughter wanted to participate in an international youth event. When I recognized how much Lisa wanted to attend this weeklong event, I had a conversation with the youth worker. I asked his input about what it would take for Lisa to go. We both agreed that the regular chaperone ratio would not meet her needs. She needed her own shadow. I quickly realized that I had to be that shadow.

We never took the attitude that Lisa had a right to participate in everything. Rather, we always worked with leadership to find what fit her best and what did not. It was part of our reality check with Lisa. They weren't easy boundaries for her to learn. But they were so important. These experiences helped her confront the implications of unchangeable limitations. It was a painful but empowering lesson.

Finding help at church

- Find out what ministries and activities already exist that will meet your child's needs and participate there first.
- Make sure that ministry leaders who work with your child have all the information they need to keep him or her safe and successful.
- Add one involvement at a time.

- Offer to provide special adaptations that make inclusion more successful.
- Find ways to support your child's leaders.
- Never recruit a person to help your child without the ministry leader's permission.
- Explain what works at home and school.
- Talk with other special-needs parents about what has worked for them at church.
- Agree on how to address behavior issues.
- If your church is interested in starting a special-needs ministry, be the first to volunteer.

Everybody needs help

I have rich experiences with people who have come alongside me or Lisa. They broke down our Jericho wall and helped us cross more than one Red Sea. They have been God's special answers to my desperate cries for help.

Sometime you can make it with a little help. Sometimes it takes a lot of help. Don't let anything stand in the way of looking for and getting help. Evaluate your strength by the way you're willing to look for help. Isolation and silence are sad ways to endure difficult times. Whether it takes a homework-helper, a support group, prayer partners, or connection with agencies and service groups who offer a variety of help, support will make a difference. It will keep you aware that the only way you can effectively meet the challenges of empowering a special-needs child is with the help of others.

Finding Help

Empowering questions

1. Where do you find the most help?
2. What prevents you from asking for help?
3. Where do you need to investigate new avenues for support?
4. How does your child ask for help? How can you encourage this skill?

Empowering strategies

- Asking for help is a sign of strength, not weakness.
- Asking for help may bring resources and people who can meet needs you can't meet.
- Ask for specific help.
- Accept the desire to help even when attempts to help fall short.
- Set clear boundaries when asking friends or family for support.
- Investigate support groups, organizations, and agencies that could offer help to your family.
- Teach a definition for independence that includes asking for help in appropriate ways and at appropriate times.

An empowering prayer

God,

You are our Helper—ever present, never late, never early.

Help me understand this truth. It's not what we want when we want it. It's what's best at the right time. When we wait for answers that don't come, remind us that we're waiting for a good reason.

We lay our needs before you, waiting for help that will come. In Jesus' name we pray.

Amen.

**If one person falls, the other can reach out
and help. But people who are alone
when they fall are in real trouble.
—Eccles. 4:10, NLT**

Empowering
Prayer

The most important lesson we have learned about praying for our son is to pray from a genuine heart.
—Les and Leslie Parrott

I asked God to make my handicapped child whole, and God said . . . her spirit is whole; her body is only temporary.
—Claudia Minden Weisz

I knew that Lisa was one new crisis away from ICU. A simmering and long undiagnosed heart infection had decimated her body. I stayed nights with her in the hospital, ready to rub an aching back, give her a drink of water, or change a cooling forehead rag. I hung on every optimistic word of her doctor. Crisis had overturned our lives—again. I canceled writing assignments, speaking engagements, Christmas shopping—everything. We were all in survival mode. Thankfully, Lisa responded to the intense antibiotic therapy. However, it further weakened her heart valves and sent us to risky heart surgery before she could regain her strength.

Nothing makes us reach for God more intensely than crisis. The truth is that in hard times we bring together everything we know about God and prayer. We don't have time to think about it. It's what we already know that helps, and it's what we don't know about God and prayer that frustrates.

> *Is prayer your steering wheel or your spare tire?*
> —Corrie ten Boom

Why is it that when prayer is the only thing we can do, we always want to do something more? We don't like to admit helplessness. It forces us to acknowledge our weakness and fear of loss. But it also invites us to rediscover God's strength and compassion and to know the difference that His presence makes.

> *The hardest thing I've ever had to do is hand our two-year-old son to the nurse who will carry him into the operating room for open-heart surgery.*
> —Martha, mother

Praying for our children at the beginning of a diagnosis, on the first day of a new school placement, about behavior issues we don't know how to handle, or during rehabilitation therapy or recovery—those are times when

Empowering Prayer

we muster everything we have ever learned about God and prayer. It's not a formula or phrasing that makes the difference. It's an authentic and very aware connection with the God who wants to heal anything that has the potential of destroying the abundant life He gives us through salvation. Sometimes it means healing a fever. More often it means healing a fear.

While everything we learn about scriptural prayer tells us that we can empty our hearts before God, prayer that only empties is half a prayer, even when it's most of the work. Praying for our children when they face difficulties requires that we learn the other half of prayer—allowing God to speak. True prayer helps us focus in ways that are not circumstantially tied. Prayer helps us know why we can commit our children's futures to the plans of a God who loves them more than we do. We can pray the prayer of Lady Julian of Norwich, that "all will be well" because we no longer insist on defining "well." We trust God's definition.

> *But all shall be well, and all shall be well,*
> *and all manner of thing shall be well.*
> —Lady Julian of Norwich

It was one of the first prayers we prayed for our children before their birth. It continues to be our priority prayer in a way that we did not anticipate. We pray for their health. We pray for their wholeness.

> *Lord, you've been faithful in the midst of each*
> *crisis we've ever had to face, and You've taught*
> *us that whatever blessings have come into our*
> *lives, your name is on the sender card.*
>
> —Martha, mother

What the Bible says

We know that healing is an integral part of the Bible. Naaman was healed of leprosy (2 Kings 5:1-14). King Hezekiah received remission for a life-threatening illness (2 Kings 20:1-7). Elijah brought the widow's son back to life (1 Kings 17:17-24). In the New Testament, Jesus healed the Canaanite woman's daughter who was "suffering terribly" (Matt. 15:21-28). He brought Jairus's daughter back to life (Mark 5:38-42). Jesus instructed the disciples to continue His healing ministry. The crippled man at the Gate Beautiful could walk after his encounter with the Lord of Peter and John (Acts 3:1-8).

Like you, I read every healing story in the Bible with a desperate desire for God to do the same for my child. I don't know why God brings healing in one place and not another. However, I've learned some important truths that have helped me find the answers God offered. I've come to realize that the healing stories in the Bible were not just about healing. They were about God's power or love or compassion or salvation. Healing helped people believe in God, not just in His healing power. I also

Empowering Prayer

learned that healing did not occur by some formula. More than anything else, healing is about connecting to God's will, action, heart, and understanding. It's about receiving what God says will heal and finding out how His will makes the critical difference.

> *I'm so glad that a mustard seed of faith is more powerful than a mountain of concern.*
> —Les, father

Some of my most life-changing lessons about prayer and God's character have come as I prayed about Lisa's health and life needs. They are lessons that continue to make me realize how prayer is my lifeline.

1. A prayer for healing is not a prayer for ease, convenience, fairness, or equality. As I began praying for Lisa, I had to admit that part of me asked for things to be easier and fairer for all of us. When I allowed God to still the storm of my struggle, He helped me become part of His calm for Lisa as well.

This helps me pray for Lisa's healing in the right priority. First, I pray for the wholeness God desires to bring. As I pray, I ask Him to examine my motives. Am I just tired of seeing her pain and frustrations? Do I want things to be easier for all of us, including me? Often I've had to take a detour and admit my needs before I could continue praying for my daughter.

2. A prayer for healing addresses eternal issues, not just temporal ones. What did Lisa need from God that would make an eternal difference in her life? She needed to know how much her Heavenly Father loved her. She needed to know His salvation and forgiveness. She needed to know that her life mattered to God. Those understandings empowered her to live a life of meaning and purpose. On the other hand, without them, even healing wouldn't make an eternal difference. That's when I began to change my prayers. I started asking God to bring the healing that would make an eternal difference. He did. Some of the healings have been emotional. Some have been spiritual. Some have been physical. Would it surprise you to know that the most important answers haven't been physical? However, all of them have brought about new levels of spiritual wholeness that enables Lisa to live the life God desires for her. Isn't that the real prayer we all pray for our children?

3. God will bring all the healing your child needs to accomplish His will. I'll never forget the occasion for this lesson. I was reading a book on small-group ministries in which the author suggested some opening questions. I read through the list until I came to this one: "What would you say to Jesus if He walked into this room and sat down beside you?" Immediately, the tears began to fall. I closed the book, because I knew I had a question. It was the same question all parents of suffering children ask: "Are you going to heal her?" I'll never forget the answer. It came through my consciousness in a way that I understood it to be God, and He said, "I *am* healing her. I'll give her all the healing she needs to do My will. Is that enough for you?"

My first response was more like "I'm not sure." I wanted Lisa to experience a pain-free and flexible body. I wanted all mental obstacles to disappear. What God was offering wasn't what I expected. That was the key. What God wanted to do in my daughter's life might not be what I expected. It might not even be what I wanted. Suddenly, this wasn't about Lisa's life. It was about mine and my trust level. Again I had to address how to submit my expectations and dreams to God. When I did, I began to see God's specific healing action in Lisa's life in subtle but transforming ways. It was an empowering prayer.

> *Jesus did not come to explain away suffering or remove it. He came to fill it with His presence.*
> —Paul Claudel

Empowering prayer

To empower our children in these often frightening and always unsettling times, we have to pray empowering prayers. Many times that means we have to start with the fears that overpower us—the "What will happen if . . ." fears, the "What else can I do?" fears. I can't pray my fears and expect an empowering result. Instead, I have to confess my fear, which usually has its root in my lack of control. I have to understand that God's control, even when I don't see it or feel it, is the operative answer.

As you pray

1. Admit your fear and helplessness. Fear is not an instrument God uses to heal or help anyone. Fear does not encourage health—it encourages more fear. That's the last thing you want your child to feel. Pray, asking God to fill you so completely with His love that there's no room for fear to stay.

Never deny your fear or any other negative feeling. Always start praying where you are, because it makes you ready to receive the first answer God wants to send. Even when you struggle with health questions that have no answers, don't start with the no-answer questions. Let God settle your heart with the overwhelming awareness that He is capably in charge. When your heart knows that the only source of true strength is from God, you'll stop trying to *be* strong. Instead, you'll pray the prayer of one who trusts God completely.

2. Pray about what you know first. God will not send help for what might happen. He's more efficient than that. He shares His help based on what *is* happening. Over and over, God counsels us to leave tomorrow's concern for tomorrow's prayers. There's enough to pray for today. Don't get ahead of reality.

> *Pray solutions, not complaints.*
>
> —Sally, parent

What are the facts: that the fever is rising, that the doctor suggested surgery, that there is no cure or answer

Empowering Prayer

today? Some facts suggest frightening scenarios. Be informed. Understand the possibilities. Research options. However, never treat the possibilities as facts before their time.

Use Phil. 4:8 as a reality-based focus to guide your prayers for your child. Where have you gotten mired in "What if?" and "If only" questions? Ask God to help you refocus on what He's doing and where He's working *now*. Ask Him to help you deal with what you know *now* so that you can prepare for what He knows will come your way tomorrow.

3. Ask God to help you cooperate with the healing He wants to bring. This has been an anchor principle for me ever since I discovered it. As I prayed for Lisa's healing, the healing of seizures and learning disabilities, the healing of arthritis and joint limitations, I became so focused on thinking about what would be better if these horrible obstacles were wiped away. I prayed desperately, specifically, and regularly about these problems. When I didn't see any changes, I didn't know what to pray. Was God not answering me? Was I not praying correctly?

Slowly, I began to see where God was working to bring His healing. It wasn't physical at first. It was emotional and spiritual healing. I began to realize that if God was starting there, I should too. The more I cooperated with God's work in Lisa's life, the more healing He brought—to both of us.

It wasn't because God was delaying the healing or

even denying it. When I was so focused on a form of healing that wouldn't make the difference God wanted to make, my struggle and frustration became part of the problem instead of part of the answer. I began to pray differently. *God, help me see where you want to bring healing. Help me cooperate with your work.* God always answered those prayers. And they always made a difference.

Where is God's healing work happening in your child? Who are instruments of that healing? How can you cooperate in those areas? Remember that God often heals a spirit before He heals a body. He may need to heal a parent's fear before He heals a child's fever. Don't second-guess where God is working. He doesn't hide His handiwork. Take time to know for sure so that you can participate in His work.

> *Prayer is not an argument with God to persuade him to move things our way, but an exercise by which we are enabled by his Spirit to move ourselves his way.* —Leonard Ravenhill

4. Pray for spiritual wholeness. Wholeness is the divine balance in an individual that does not depend on circumstances. It is the healthy integration of mind, body, and spirit. Remember that when Jesus healed the woman with the bleeding disorder, He said He had made her "whole" (Matt. 9:22, KJV). Make spiritual wholeness your focus, and let God continue to teach you what it means for your child.

Empowering Prayer

The big question

"What do you say to a child who asks 'Why did God make me this way?'" As I looked into the eyes of the mother who asked it, I knew it was her question as well. It was part accusation and part plea. I put my arm around her shoulder to acknowledge her grief. I told her that there's no satisfying answer to her question to take away her hurt or help her feel OK about the hardship and inequities she and her child face.

God does not create the suffering or disability. Our fallen world does that. Instead, we go to God with our brokenness, our confusion, our questions, and ask Him to bring purpose and growth *out of it*. We change our "Why?" questions to "How?" questions. We affirm the unique characteristics that He *did* create and find out how He created them to be part of His answer. We submit the part of the question we don't understand so that we can live the answers He *does* give.

> *When he grasped the idea that he is God's creation and the Lord loves him this way and has a plan for him, he was able to get past being angry at God.* —Lynne, parent

Empowering prayer models

Three empowering prayer models have been important to me. Each comes from Scripture. Every time I've used one of these models, I've learned how much more available God is than I ever imagined. I learned that however He responded to my prayer gave me what I didn't know I needed. Sometimes it was as simple as sending someone with whom I could share my struggles. Sometimes He answered with an instruction or opened a way that did not exist before. These prayers continue to teach me that the goal of prayer is to get *to* God, not to get something out of Him.

Four-corner prayer

It was Christmas Eve. We planned to drive halfway to my parents' house after the Christmas Eve service. I had already packed bags, presents, and goodies to add to Christmas dinner. Then it happened. Lisa started having seizures. They were small, exactly like the ones she experienced the last time we had followed the doctor's orders to take her off of her medication.

Immediately, I sent out a plea to my prayer partners. Mark brought back a message that I keep in my heart to this day. "Don't worry. Each of us has a corner of Lisa's mat. We'll carry her to Jesus." I put that message in my pocket and fingered it often until I could connect with Lisa's doctor.

I call it "four-corner prayer." It comes from the story in Luke 5:17-19 about the four friends who carried their friend to Jesus. In the middle of a crisis, I have to be the problem-solver, the nurturer, the calmer, the make-

Empowering Prayer

it-happen person. Often there's not time for anything but quick cries to God. That's when I need "mat-carriers"—four prayer partners who agree to carry my child to Jesus when I don't have the energy to do it. It releases me to do a parent's work in the middle of crisis. It calms me to know that four trusted heart-friends are praying.

Enlist the prayer support of your own "mat-carriers" for everything from homework struggles to doctors' appointments. Ask them to pray about medication choices and counseling sessions. Take comfort in the fact that their prayers also carry you to Jesus.

Four-corner prayer partners

- Ask four friends or two couples to be your spiritual intercessors.
- Meet with them, and read the story in Luke 5:17-19.
- Ask these friends to be "mat-carriers" for you and your child.
- Ask each to sign one corner of a 3 x 5 card and put their phone number on the back.
- Ask one of the four to be your contact who calls the others when there's a prayer need.
- Close by standing in the center with each mat carrier at a corner around you. Ask each to pray for you and your child.
- Keep the card in a prominent place.

Lord, help me!

The story of the woman who brought her daughter's suffering to Jesus holds great meaning for me. Every special-needs parent understands the depth of that mother's pain, because nothing hurts us more than our own children's pain. It doesn't have to be physical pain that causes our children to suffer. Teasing, social struggles, and isolation cause suffering just as great as anything a pain censor records.

Every time I read this story I'm amazed that this mother asked for mercy for herself before she asked help for her daughter. Read it for yourself in Matt. 15:21-28. She interrupted Jesus while He was in retreat. Before introducing herself or presenting her need, she asked for His mercy. Then, when the disciples tried to get rid of her, she reworded her plea: "Lord, help *me!*" (v. 25, emphasis added).

It wasn't a selfish request. Instead of denying her own needs, she brought them to Jesus. And she brought them first. I find that very reassuring. In fact, I've learned that it is critical for me to bring my needs to Jesus first. If I don't, my needs get in the way. My fear can push my child too hard. I can act out of my own pain and push away the very people who could help. If I continue to treat my pain as less important than my child's pain, I run the risk of becoming an obstacle that God has to work around rather than an instrument He can use.

Empowering Prayer

"Lord, help me" is not a selfish prayer when your child is in need. It's an empowering prayer. It gives God permission to confront any emotion, perception, or thought that gets in the way of the answer He's preparing. Pray it with the confidence that God has an answer on the way.

The Mary-Martha prayer

Another prayer I learned to pray early is the "Mary-Martha prayer." It comes from the story of Lazarus. When Mary and Martha knew that Lazarus was desperately ill, the scripture says that they sent word to Jesus. Their message was simple: "Lord, the one you love is sick" (John 11:3). They didn't diagnose his illness or tell Jesus what to do. For me, the request emphasizes that they trusted Jesus to know what to do with the one who was sick.

It's so easy to get stuck on what I think should happen. Whether it's a school issue, health issue, job issue, relationship issue, speech issue, or mobility issue, I go into overtime thinking how to solve a problem. But Jesus doesn't need my counsel—He needs my obedience.

When I don't know what else to pray, I simply call upon the embracing love of God for my child and say, "Lord, the one you love is sick [frustrated, depressed, struggling]." It's a prayer that affirms my trust in God's ability to do the right thing at the right time.

Teach your child to pray

Praying empowering prayers *for* your children is only one part of the equation. Teaching your children to pray empowering prayers for themselves is your real goal. While some spiritually sensitive children demonstrate more trust than their parents, most children mirror the trust of their parents. Ask yourself this question: "If my child prays as I do for the rest of his [her] life, how will those prayers empower?"

If my child prays as I do for the rest of his [her] life, how will those prayers empower?

Use the following ideas to become prayer partners with your child. Learn from the innocence and willing trust of your child. Share your lessons about God and prayer. Begin a journey that will carry you far past childhood.

1. Teach your child to ask God to reveal His purpose for his or her life. I hope you've come to understand that the disability is not "the purpose." The disability, like any other life boundary, is a tool you can use to discover God's purpose. As a context-defining description, it tells you where you will find God's purpose and where you will not. Emphasize that God's love is not based on what your child can or can't do. Your child exists because of God's love. The best way to respond to that love is to cooperate with God's will. This means that life for a special-needs child is not about changing what he or she can't do. It's about discovering what your child can do as he or she follows God.

2. Teach your child to wait for God's answer. Teaching your child to wait for God's answer means *you* have to wait first. You have to be willing not to run ahead of God with your own ideas or pronouncements as you talk with your child. Nothing will bind the two of you together more quickly than learning how to wait on God *together*. Besides, when your child recognizes that you don't have all the answers and must depend on God to supply them, it teaches him or her to do the same.

Also understand that God enjoys direct communication. He shares His plan with the person who will live it. As parents, we may sense His plans for our children because of what we know; however, God knows how to deliver His messages in uniquely personal ways. Our job as empowering parents is to nurture the sensitivity that makes it possible for our children to hear the message for themselves.

3. Teach your child to be honest with God. Accept whatever emotion your child has. It's healthful to express emotions. It's immature to act them out. That's why we need to help our children learn the vocabulary, the pictures, or the sign language that communicates real emotion. We need to encourage them to express these emotions to God as well as to parents or friends. Keep some scripture handy to emphasize how people in the Bible expressed their emotions to God. Talk about how to express feelings without hurting anybody with them.

Scriptures about emotions

- Cain expressed anger inappropriately with violence (Gen. 4:4-8).
- King Ahab expressed his emotions in an immature way (1 Kings 21:4-6).
- When Nehemiah expressed his sadness, he received an answer that changed his disposition (Neh. 2:1-8).
- Nehemiah expressed his anger appropriately to right a wrong (Neh. 5:6-12).
- The rich man kept his sad feelings to himself (Matt. 19:22).
- The Bible encourages us to express our feelings (James 5:13).
- Good reminders—Prov. 29:22; Eph. 4:26

4. Teach your child how to listen to God. Learning how to recognize God's voice is a process. The first and easiest way to teach children to recognize God's voice is with Scripture. Find some simple verses, and identify the week as a listening-to-God week. Make it an adventure for the whole family. At the end of the week, let everyone share how a scripture or Bible story made him or her think differently about a choice or attitude. That's God speaking. It doesn't get any simpler than that.

5. Pray with your child regularly. Some parents find it easier to pray *for* their children than to pray *with* them. This is where we demonstrate that our relation-

Empowering Prayer

ship with God is intimate and satisfying. Ask your child how you can pray for a specific issue. Ask him or her to pray for you as well. Nothing has touched me more deeply than when my daughter prayed for me.

Pray about everything

Phil. 4:6 reminds us to pray about everything. Nothing is too trivial for prayer. Nothing is too impossible. Pray when the ideas don't work, and pray when they do. Pray when things are going well, and when nothing is right. Make prayer your bridge to God. Make it your first response to problems. Trust God's answer before it comes, before you can even name it. Let prayer prepare your heart for whatever answer God wants to bring, because whatever God adds makes more difference than our best idea.

Empowering questions

1. When you pray for your child, do you spend as much time listening to God as talking to Him? How can you address any imbalance?

2. Who are your "mat-carriers"?

3. Where do you need to pray, "Lord, help me"?

4. How are you teaching your child to pray for himself or herself?

5. Using the following scriptures, write a prayer for spiritual wholeness for your child: Deut. 5:29; 6:5; Prov. 13:12; Col. 1:9-14; 1 Thess. 5:23.

Empowering strategies

- Realize that the prayer for healing is not a formula.
- Admit your fear and helplessness.
- Pray about what you know first.
- Ask God to help you cooperate with the healing/answer He wants to bring.
- Pray for spiritual wholeness.
- Pray for God's mercy.
- Pray the "Mary-Martha prayer."

An empowering prayer

Great Physician,

The one you love is sick. And frankly, Lord, it's not just our child. We suffer too. We ask for your presence and wisdom for every doctor's appointment and as a part of every medical regimen. Help us see your healing work, even when it's in places we don't believe will make much difference. Since you love our child more than we can, we submit our hope for healing to your unfailing love.

Afraid of everything but you, we pray in your name.

Amen.

**The LORD is near to all who call on him,
to all who call on him in truth.
—Ps. 145:18**

Flying
Lessons

Our goal is for our boys to live as independent and fulfilling a life as possible. What that means, I'm not really sure.
—John, parent

On love's wings, children dare to learn to fly.
—Melissa England

Lisa sat in her favorite rocker in her very first apartment. The dream that seemed impossible during high school and felt permanently postponed after heart surgery surprised both of us with its bittersweet reality. We had spent the week moving in her furniture and organizing drawers, closets, and cupboards. Caring friends gave her a housewarming, and there were a lot of new items to decorate her two-room apartment. It was her dream come true. There hadn't been many accessible dreams in the arduous journey to this moment.

Before I left her alone to savor her first night, I held her hands in mine and prayed a prayer of thanksgiving and protection. We both cried. They were tears of joy as well as fear. Could she make it on her own? Was this going to be another broken dream? We wouldn't know unless we gave it a try.

The way we hugged good-bye, you would have thought we were moving hundreds of miles apart. As I walked to the car, I remembered the numberless times Lisa had asked, "Mom, do you think I'll ever be able to live on my own?" I gave her the same answer I did when she wondered if she would graduate from high school. "I don't know. We'll just have to find out." I thought about how we had arrived at this moment. It certainly wasn't by accident.

An early start

Since the beginning, we've continued to adapt, brainstorm, and experiment with processes that helped Lisa achieve a level of independence appropriate for her limitations. I had to keep asking, "*Can* she do this?" Then we had to find the answer. I don't even remember how many ways she tried to put on her socks by herself before we found the process that worked. Lisa wasn't always excited about independence in daily living skills even when she wanted the skill for her future. I constantly had to encourage without nagging. I didn't always succeed.

Flying Lessons

Empowering independence

- Find out what your child wants to do independently, and start there.
- List the independent skills necessary to achieve future goals, and start with the most basic.
- Break a new goal into very small, manageable steps.
- Allow time for adequate practice before beginning a new goal.
- Affirm. Affirm! *Affirm!*
- Monitor mastery by how much cueing your child needs to use the skill.
- Celebrate any level of achievement.

It's important to start early, because our children don't assimilate independent living skills as easily as those without disabilities and special needs. Our children need ample opportunities to learn how to make appropriate choices within their mental and physical health boundaries. While children are young, parents expect to coach independence skills. The problem comes when we realize that we're still coaching some of the same skills long after other children their age have mastered them. It's a never-ending objective.

> *Bike-riding is something our boys do well. We give them freedom to ride by themselves around town. I believe they need to have opportunities to do what they enjoy and learn from it.*
> —John, parent

Commit yourself to learn what coaching strategies work. Commit to experimenting with organizational tools that make a difference. Practice the kind of communication that motivates best. Most of all, find ways to turn responsibility over to your child to use the strategy. No matter how well an idea works, it's worthless if your child never takes the initiative to use it without your cueing. This transfer of responsibility is what empowering is all about. It identifies how committed you are to empowering your child for the future.

My most important lesson
—From special-needs parents

- Realizing the immense opportunity I have to influence my child. —Lynne

- God never allows you to have more than you can handle. —John

- Seeing how the Lord had His hand in everything and trusting that He will be faithful. —Lynne

- God cares for our son more than we could. —Sarah

- My personal "trust factor" has been greatly enhanced through this experience. —Lynne

- God will show you a way through the dark valley, even when it appears like a black hole that threatens to swallow both you and your child. —Sarah

Start with small portions of power to make decisions. Allow your child to experience the full consequences of those decisions. If we give our children the power to make their own decisions but protect them from consequences, we destine them to a roller-coaster life fraught with minor and major crises. The downside of this process for any parent is that we experience the consequences of our children's consequences.

Most of the time enabling is nothing more than an exercise in self-protection. *We* don't want to experience the embarrassment of the temper tantrum or the accident that requires a trip home to change underwear, and so *we* do everything *we* can to prevent them—sometimes quite successfully. It's so tempting to protect ourselves under the misguided belief that we're protecting our children. Look at the choices your child makes outside of your care. That's where you evaluate successful empowerment.

An ounce of prevention

For many of our children, independence involves preventing problems. Lisa was an accident waiting to happen when she left the house with several items divided between both hands trying to open a door or get into the car without dropping something. I showed her how to group things better. I encouraged her to take a book bag for extra items. Finally, I made it a rule with consequences if she broke it. Most of the time she thought it was just one of those unnecessary Mom rules. Now that she lives by herself with no one to pick up the items she drops, she understands the importance of prevention.

Learn the strategies that prevent unnecessary problems or emergencies. Usually some level of organization tops the list. The skill for a child to understand body signals is not always automatic and must be taught. Even emotional outbursts come from somewhere. Learning what the triggers are and how to use them to prevent inappropriate behavior can be as monumental as learning to read. Ask a special education teacher for specific ideas to prevent a recurring problem. As much as possible, turn these strategies over to your child.

Realize that children (or parents) in denial aren't ready to accept responsibility for preventing problems. Before you can adopt a strategy to prevent a problem, you have to accept that there *is* a problem. Over and over I had to reassure Lisa that recognizing a problem is a good thing. It wasn't about adding something she couldn't do to an ever-growing list. It was a way to find out what she *could* do.

Skill by skill

When Lisa entered her last years of high school, before we knew whether independent living was within her reach, she began to take on one skill of independent living at a time. In the summer she was responsible for her own breakfast and lunch, because she preferred a schedule that was different from the rest of us. She learned to use the microwave. Once a week we added at least one simple food-preparation idea. She made Jell-O, soup, and microwave brownies. She also learned to take responsibility for her own laundry, learning one category of wash at a time. We both learned that she worked best in a set routine. That's when we began to talk through a schedule for the week or a special day. We learned to write it down. To this day, Lisa handles independent life well when she knows there's a plan. Without it, change overwhelms and stresses her to the point of experiencing physical consequences. She's had to learn that it's best to ask for help *before* the stress sets in. She continues to learn that asking for help at the right time keeps her independent and successful.

Start your own skill list. Be careful about overestimating or underestimating your child's realistic abilities. Start with 100-percent reachable goals before graduating to more challenging ones. It doesn't matter how long it takes to master a new skill. Empowerment doesn't come with time limits. And remember—there's little empowerment in a process that pushes your child to the point of frustration. Ask me how I know.

> *Be very aware of your child's limitations.*
> *Build trust before difficult situations arise.*
> —Heidi, adult

Life after school

Special-education services can follow your child until he or she is 21. There's a great deal of comfort in knowing that. However, it's never too early to think about life after individual education plans. In fact, it's what happens *after* the school services end that most clearly identifies how committed you are to empowering your child to live the most appropriate level of independence possible.

Again, it's all about starting early. Find out what services your child can receive and for how long. Ask about the services that support a child afterward. Do some research. In my Web research I found some very helpful checklists that addressed transitioning from adolescence to adulthood. They can help you identify what level of support your child will need in order to live as independently as is realistically possible.

> *I wondered—would he be a productive member of society?*
> —Heather, parent

What will life after school look like? Will there be a job? Will it be full time? Will there be an apartment or group home? How will your child want to spend leisure time? What level of independent transportation will your child be able to access? How much financial or other support will you continue to provide? How much can others supply? While these questions may overwhelm you as you send your child off to elementary school, keep them in the back of your head. Don't postpone them too long. Waiting too late to answer these questions puts you and your child at risk for frustration and making desperate decisions.

Finding a life goal

Getting through school isn't why God created your child. However, when school issues fill the present and future, it's easy to act as if it's your one goal in life. Think beyond school. What is God's purpose for your child? School helps identify skills and provides knowledge, but it can't identify God's purpose. Neither can you. Finding God's purpose is a personal discovery that your child must make. You can affirm, encourage, and suggest, but you can't determine God's purpose for your child. God will communicate His will to anyone who listens. Encourage your child to do the listening and trust God's ability to speak.

> *Help your child find a vision for life.*
> —Sally, parent

A life goal is more than finding an answer to the question "What will I do after school?" It's about making a contribution to a larger circle of influence. That contribution can be as simple as sharing an innocent and uncomplicated perspective with people who have forgotten how to relish the simple joys of life. It may involve a job but must be defined in a broader way than a job description. It may involve volunteer work or simply the creative use of the hours in a day. God knows how to match goals with the challenges your child faces. His goal is reachable and will not overwhelm.

More than once I've had to realign what I hoped was God's plan for Lisa. My goals frustrated her and often came out of my fears about her future. When I surrendered my specific desires so that I could become a tool for God to use to deliver His own message directly to her and not through me, both of us had fewer struggles.

Keep an updated résumé

Identifying employable skills for your child becomes a crucial issue during high school. While vocational rehabilitation services are helpful, they have limits. No one can guarantee a job for your child. Community jobs and resources may limit what they can offer. Their client base may force them to specialize in certain kinds of jobs that may or may not meet your child's needs. That's why starting a résumé early is a good idea. Keep thinking about job skills that come from volunteer work, school, and church involvement.

It was difficult for us to see Lisa's employable skills. We started with her interests. Lisa's love of children made her a good volunteer in our church's children's ministry. From that interest she explored daycare as a part of her vocational training in high school. We found out that it takes more than a love for children to perform work as a paid employee. It was valuable information and led us to remove childcare from her job list possibilities while keeping it a priority in volunteer work.

One of the goals of your child's individual education plan should be creating a résumé. Depending on
the services he or she receives, it could be up to you and
your child to keep the résumé updated after high school.
Keep it on your computer, and update it after each
birthday or after new experiences.

Make a notebook or file

I keep a file with a multitude of resources available
at my fingertips. This is an independent living file that's
different from the medical notebook I described in chapter 5. I keep information about her caregivers, her daily
schedule, a sample grocery shopping list, a sample
week's menu, a packing list, a catalog for adaptive
equipment, and her work information, including job description and résumé. At the front, I keep the most updated report of her caseworker's annual review. This is a
good place to keep any other information that affects
your child's daily life.

While researching resources for independent living, I
found an idea that took the notebook even further. It's a
way for your child to gather the details that are important for anyone who supplies support. This could include
a picture gallery of friends and family. It can include information about your child's special challenges in his or
her own words. Add a page each for specific interests,
food preferences, sleep preferences, the way to give support, any pet peeves, and other information that your

child feels is important. Encourage your child to decorate the front cover in a way that describes who he or she is. The idea is to incorporate as much of your child's personality as possible while supplying information that you as family often take for granted. I'm in the process of helping Lisa build one that includes her morning routine, what substitute caregivers need to know about helping her into a car and crossing streets. It shares where she needs help and where she needs an opportunity to maintain independence.

Finding a place to call home

Perhaps the most important question you and your child will address is where he or she will live away from parents. It's easy to be so focused on *how* they'll live that we forget to address *where* they'll live. Most of the time our children will develop more skills of independent living away from us. No matter how independent we try to make our children, all parents give in to doing too much. Away from us, they may finally learn how to take full responsibility for the kind of life they want to live.

Talk to other parents who have researched options for their young adult children. Ask the special education personnel what the options are in your community. Call and ask to make a visit. Learn what the waiting lists are like and how to make an application. Gather the information even if you don't know if you need it. This is especially critical for a Christian family. We investigated

some situations in which the resident mix did not provide the same kind of positive atmosphere in which Lisa
grew up. This made our search for the right independent
living situation more complicated.

Finding a place to live

- Research possibilities within your community.
- Visit them and make a priority list.
- Find out what exists within a 50- to 100-mile ra-
  dius as well.
- Determine what level of support your child needs
  to live in different options.
- Ask other parents of special-needs young adults
  about their experiences.
- Use all the information to help you identify the
  independent-living skills your child will need.
- When your child begins to ask questions about
  life after school, offer your information in small
  doses.
- The year before your child is ready for a move,
  visit the best options as a family.
- Keep communication open with your child.
- Maintain realistic goals without destroying your
  child's spirit.

Yo-yo experiences

I think we knew that getting Lisa into an apartment
was not the end of our intense investment into her life.

Her limitations require ongoing support. Sometimes she just needs reassurance that she's doing the right thing. At other times it means she needs us at a doctor's appointment or for a shopping trip, since buying clothing is never simple. She's had to recuperate from health crises with us when she needed 24-hour support.

The first time she came home for a long recuperation, I think we all wondered if it was the end of independent living. Now I understand these incidents as yo-yo times. While we expect them to be temporary, we always know that something could change that. They require flexibility, patience, and adaptability from all of us. And they also require clear boundaries. Set boundaries to address potential conflict areas. It could involve television, kitchen, bathroom clean-up, or laundry rules. Life doesn't return to where it was before your child moved out. All of you are at a different place. That's where the tension comes. Don't be afraid to clear the air. Talk about your concerns before you lay down rules. Offer options and invite input. Communicate your desire to protect the independence that your child has mastered while protecting family rights.

A chance to succeed

If we're to complete our responsibilities as parents of special-needs children, we must honor our children by giving them an opportunity to try their own wings. That doesn't mean pushing them into a world in which

they've not been prepared to live. We must give them the
tools it takes to learn the skills of independent living that
match their abilities.

> *Find opportunities for them to be successful.*
> —John, parent

It also involves letting them fail when they do it
their own way. If we want to give them a chance to succeed, they'll also have to taste failure. Few successes occur without trial and error. Many times I've had to come
alongside Lisa to remind her, "You didn't do it wrong—
you just learned what doesn't work. Let's use that lesson
to help us create a different way."

> *Create an environment that enables children to*
> *feel success in a situation that might otherwise*
> *defeat them.*   —Heidi, adult

As much as possible, build into every independent
trial enough support to ensure success. The first week in
Lisa's apartment, she called us every morning when she
got up, every afternoon when she returned from work,
and every night before she went to bed. The next week,
we reduced it. The next week we reduced it further. Now
she's back to calling every day, because it's her idea.

In our relationship with Lisa, we've tried to build
connection that meets her needs while providing an ac-
ceptable level of accountability. That will vary from child

to child. If a child perceives it as control, it won't do anything for the relationship.

Some of our children may function better away from us than with us. We may not have the ability to provide the consistent and highly structured routine they need. We may not be able to meet their physical or emotional needs in a home environment. This doesn't make you a bad parent. Empowerment is about releasing a child to live successfully, wherever that means.

Planning for the future

There's one last issue that all parents of special-needs children should address. What will happen to your child without you? No one expects to outlive his or her children. That makes it even more crucial to make a definite life plan that protects your special-needs child in every way. Get appropriate legal and financial counsel when you make these decisions. Talk to your other children. Assume nothing. Know what your options are so that you can choose the best plan. Make your decisions prayerfully, asking for God's very specific direction. Make a plan even if you have to change it.

Empowering obstacles

- Fear, resentment, bitterness, denial, and over-protectiveness. —Louann, adult
- Fear, which leads to enabling. —Theresa, learning specialist

- Feeling sorry for the child and letting him or her get away with things. —Darlene, parent
- Lack of understanding, creativity, and diligence. —Heidi, adult

Empowered to live God's dream

"Mom, you know when I decided to live, don't you?"

Lisa's words sent a chill through my body. I didn't know that life was up for decision. I asked her to explain, and she recounted the days before her heart surgery. We spent a week waiting for the right surgeon to return, and she was as near death as I ever want to see her. But that's not what forced the decision. The artificial valves that would save her life would make bearing children a life-threatening possibility. I did not realize the impact of that in Lisa's life. She still held tightly to every girl's dream of marriage and children while I had long since seen it as something that would never happen. Heart surgery forced her to give up that hope. At that time she thought it would be easier to die instead.

"I had to trust that God's dream was better than mine." Lisa explained. "I decided I wanted to live to find out what He wanted to do with my life."

It was an empowering moment for her. That's when I knew that our commitment to empower had paid off. On her own, she was choosing God to direct her life. There is no higher empowerment choice than that.

As you seek to empower your child, understand

that God has dreamed a dream big enough to motivate your child for life. The physical, mental, and emotional challenges that your child faces are not obstacles for God. He never dreams a dream that's outside our reach. Perhaps we should consider ourselves fortunate to have to learn this lesson so specifically. We can leave nothing to chance. Every day is another opportunity to empower for life. Every day is another chance to find the dream that God has dreamed and become partners with Him to make it come true. While empowering is not a formula to guarantee that our children will choose God and His dream, other options can do more to prevent it.

Step back often. Review God's desire to empower you. Lean on His wisdom. Remember that hope is always the last word, and God gives it. He wants to empower you to parent your child successfully according to His definition of success. He doesn't promise easy outs or quick fixes. He's with you for the long run. His main concern is to help all of you make it to the finish line, where He can enjoy you in ways you cannot even imagine. Never forget that Phil. 1:6 provides the best foundation to keep on empowering, because "he who began a good work in you will carry it on to completion."

Make every day an empowering one for you and your child.

Empowering questions:

1. How am I encouraging independence in my child? Where do I need to encourage it more?

2. What preventive strategies does my child need to adopt? Who can help me identify them and implement them?

3. What questions about my child's future do I need to begin to research?

4. How can I encourage my child to discover a life goal?

Empowering strategies

- Start early teaching and nurturing independence.
- Find coaching strategies that work.
- Prevent unnecessary crises with effective strategies.
- Make a list of independent living skills, and begin to teach one skill at a time, one small step at a time.
- Begin collecting information about future independent-living possibilities.
- Help your child identify God's purpose for his or her life.
- Give children a chance to fail and a strategy for learning from it.
- Celebrate God's dream for your child.

An empowering prayer

God,

You have designed my child's life. There is no disability, disease, or limitation that can prevent it. Your creativity and resources are enough to help my child find purpose, significance,

and fulfillment. Remind me that there's no "might have been."
There's only this reality. And into this reality your best work
blooms. I commit myself again to what you want to accomplish in
my child and in us.

Anticipating in your name.

Amen.

> **He who began a good work in you**
> **will carry it on to completion.**
> **—Phil. 1:6**

Appendix

How to Start a Faith-Based Support Group

- Identify the purpose of your support group and its relationship to your local church.
- Speak with the appropriate ministry leader about your idea and confirm accountability issues.
- Recruit a core leadership group.
- Make a job description for each person (such as communications, publicity, resources, host/hostess, and so on).
- Make a recruitment list.
- Consider whether you want to provide childcare.
- Identify the basics. When will you meet? Where will you meet? How often will you meet?
- Consider a name for your support group.
- Decide how to provide support in between meetings.
- Set a first meeting date, publicize it, and send out invitations.

Tips for Running a Faith-Based Support Group

- Arrange chairs in a circle to promote intercommunication.
- Be the first to welcome each person who arrives.
- Start on time. End on time.
- Pass around a sign-up sheet for contact information.
- Share your empowering vision/purpose for the group.
- Identify how faith in God is your foundation for support and help.
- Go around the circle asking each person/new person to share his or her name, family information, and anything else about his or her journey as a special-needs parent.
- Redirect communication if someone seems to monopolize sharing.
- Keep communication focused on empowering strategies.
- Protect against negative spirals.
- Communicate your confidentiality standard.
- Take time to pray each time someone shares a need. Make it a twofold prayer: one for the child and one for the parent(s).
- Use the empowering questions at the end of each chapter to stimulate discussion around a chapter subject.

- Consider occasionally asking a professional to make a short presentation or be available for questions.
- Share a verse that has empowered you on your journey.
- Always end with prayer.
- Don't expect consistent attendance.
- Share results with ministry leaders regularly.

Starting a Special-needs Ministry

- Dream with ministry leaders about adding this ministry to your church.
- Visit a church that already has a special-needs ministry in place.
- Check out curriculum and other available resources.
- Identify a space and time.
- Plan a timeline with intermediate steps (such as personnel, mailing list, curriculum, budget request, and so on), and submit it to ministry leaders.
- Submit a proposed recruitment list to ministry leaders.
- Prepare a mission statement.
- Announce the new ministry to the church.
- Prepare a brochure that identifies the mission and scope of the ministry you plan to offer.
- Identify a medical emergency plan and emergency evacuation plan.
- Assess your church's accessibility. Check entrances, ways to get to the classroom, restrooms, sanctuary, and any other place where a special-needs child needs access.
- Survey your church's constituency to find who needs this ministry. Address these needs first.

- Enlist prayer supporters, helpers, teachers, and any skilled personnel who will make your ministry safe and effective.
- Identify a basic child-to-helper/teacher ratio, and agree to maintain that ratio even if it means keeping a waiting list. Check with agencies or school personnel who can help you identify the safest ratio.
- Schedule a training day for all volunteers and other resource people.
- Set a date and begin enrollment.
- One week before the first session, meet with all personnel for prayer. Pray for each child, worker, parent, and support person. Pray that each child and parent will feel valued and loved. Dedicate the future of the ministry to God.
- Enjoy the first session, and look forward to a fulfilling ministry.

Ways to Prepare Your Church for a Special-needs Ministry

- Write an announcement for your church newsletter.
- Ask a parent or other individual with a special challenge to talk about how this ministry will make a difference for children and their parents.
- Ask a counselor or teacher who works with these families to share with the congregation.

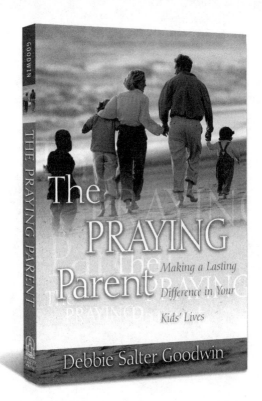

Also from Debbie Salter Goodwin

The most important gift you can give your child is prayer. Learning to pray the right prayers for your child can result in the transformation of your heart and mind as well as the heart and mind of your child.

The Praying Parent
Making a Lasting Difference in Your Kids' Lives
By Debbie Salter Goodwin

ISBN-13: 978-0-8341-2176-8

Available from Beacon Hill Press

Learn to nuture skills in your children that will foster their ability to develop healthy relationships with others and authentic relationships with God.

These seven skills provide a foundation for your child to learn to communicate and relate to you and to utlimately worship God and build a relationship with Him. Each skill involves controlling and using emotion to enhance relationships at home, school, and church.

7 Emotional Skills Every Child Needs
By Pam Galbraith and Rachel C. Hoyer

ISBN-13: 978-0-8341-2049-5

Available wherever Christian books are sold.

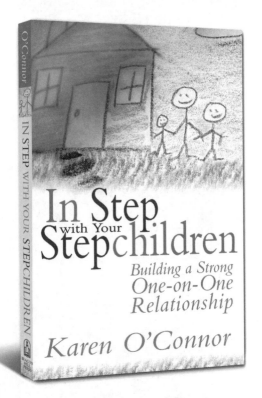

Available from Beacon Hill Press

In Step with Your Stepchildren equips stepparents with the emotional and spiritual tools needed to build loving relationships with their stepchildren, regardless of the circumstances.

Learn to take advantage of the unique challenges and opportunities you have as a stepparent to influence the life of your stepchild.

In Step with Your Stepchildren
Building a Strong One-on-One Relationship
By Karen O'Conner

ISBN-13: 978-0-8341-2045-7